THE LIFE OF MOZART

Copyright © 1968 by Residenz Verlag, Salzburg
This translation © 1969 by Macmillan & Company Ltd and St Martin's Press Inc.

Published by
MACMILLAN & COMPANY LTD
Little Essex St., London W.C. 2, and also at Bombay, Calcutta and Madras.
Macmillan South Africa (Publishers) Pty Ltd, Johannesburg
The Macmillan Company of Canada Ltd, Toronto
The Macmillan Company of Australia Pty Ltd, Melbourne
ST MARTIN'S PRESS INC., 175 Fifth Avenue, New York 10010
Library of Congress catalog card number 68-8445
Printed in Austria by F. Sochor, Zell am See

The Life of MOZART

An account in text and pictures

by

HANS CONRAD FISCHER

and

LUTZ BESCH

MACMILLAN

London · Toronto · Melbourne

ST MARTIN'S PRESS
New York
1969

FOREWORD

The authors of a book on Mozart can today offer few new facts, but must rely mainly on a new and fresh presentation of the rich material at hand. Few of Mozart's admirers can acquire all the many volumes on his life and music, and we offer, therefore, this study of Mozart in pictures and text. It is not a new interpretation of the music, but a simple account which we hope will appeal to the general reader.

The Life of Mozart is derived in part from the film of the same name, which was the first full-length film treatment of the composer's life to be made. During the preparation of the film we spent a year travelling through nine countries photographing the various places associated with Mozart's life and works, and revisiting localities historically linked with him. As in the film, our main concern in this book has been for the significant detail — for instance the face, and the expression, are the most important features of a person and we have therefore often preferred to reproduce part of a portrait rather than the whole. We have quoted only the most important passages from Mozart's letters, those of his family and friends, and from the numerous petitions, diaries and newspaper articles, and have everywhere brought punctuation and spelling up to date. The various documents relating to Mozart's life are freely available in scholarly editions and those readers who wish to inform themselves more fully can refer to the standard texts mentioned at the end of this book.

Many myths and false conceptions surround the life of Mozart, but today we feel that it should be possible to see him through his work, and through his writings and those of his contemporaries, in an objective, lively and immediate way that owes nothing to the over-sentimental approach of previous generations. Unfortunately, in every book about Mozart the most essential thing must be absent — his music; but we hope that lovers of Mozart and his works may find this account in words and pictures of interest and value.

5

When we hear the name Mozart we think only of one man, but it is not a rare name. Any modern street or telephone directory, in Bavaria, for instance, shows dozens of Mozarts: bank clerks, crane drivers, furriers, post office clerks, shopkeepers, factory workers, all listed under that name. We need only go to Augsburg, where people called Mozart have lived for generations, the city where at one time the Imperial Diet of the Holy Roman Empire sat.

The first of the composer's ancestors to live there was David Mozart who went to the city in the middle of the seventeenth century, but the name is much older than that. It is found in early documents, variously spelt — Motzart, Motzet and Motzahart. What may be the first mention occurs in 1331 when a farmer of that name had land at Fischachauf about twenty kilometres south-west of Augsburg. From then on the name appears again and again in over twenty villages in central Swabia.

David Mozart was not the first to move into the Imperial city. A painter called Christoph Mozart was there as early as 1567. Later another painter, Anton Mozart, contributed to the artistic development of the city. A certain Johannes Mozart was abbot of the monastery of the Holy Cross.

The name of David Mozart first appears on the Burgess Roll of Augsburg on 17 January 1643. He had been apprenticed as a mason, became a master mason and was for a time the head of the Masons' Guild. He had moved within the city walls from a nearby village to the west. He acquired a house in the Jacob district. He married Maria Negele of Lechhausen, a village just east of the town. One of their sons, Michael, became a Franciscan friar but three others were masons like their father.

Franz, the composer's grandfather, was cast out from the Masons' Guild because he had helped to bury the body of an illegitimate man, an assistant executioner, which in those days was a reprehensible deed. He remained a pauper for the rest of his life. The records show that he became an inmate of the workhouse at the age of thirty-three. The Augsburg workhouse, the 'Fuggerei' as it is called, was the earliest institution of its kind. It had been founded by the wealthy merchants Jakob and Anton Fugger who 'in a spirit of graciousness' made this refuge 'for citizens who were honest but afflicted with poverty'.

Franz Mozart — 'honest but afflicted with poverty' — married Anna Harrer, who is said to have been born at Obernbuch or Oberpüchrhain. When he died, at the age of forty-five, he left three children. The eldest, Johann Georg, became a bookbinder. He had no children by his first wife, but later married Anna Maria Sulzer, the daughter of a weaver who had moved to Augsburg from Baden. Research has not yet established which Baden this was, but it was probably the one in Markgrafschaft where the name Sulzer is frequently to be found in the records of that time.

On 14 November 1719, their first child Johann Georg Leopold Mozart was born. Eight other children were born between 1720 and 1735 — five boys and three girls.

David Mozart	Maria Negele
Mason from Pfersee	from Lechhausen
d. 1685 in Augsburg	d. 1697 in Augsburg

Franz Mozart	Anna Harrer
Mason	from Obernbuch (Oberpüchrhain)
b. 1649 in Augsburg	d. in Augsburg

Johann Georg Mozart	Anna Maria Sulzer
Bookbinder	
b. 1679 in Augsburg	b. 1696 in Augsburg
d. 1736 in Augsburg	d. 1766 in Augsburg

Johann Georg Leopold Mozart
Episcopal Vice-Kapellmeister
b. 14. 11. 1719 in Augsburg
d. 28. 5. 1787 in Salzburg

The child Leopold Mozart was sent first to the primary school at St. Ulrich, and later to the Jesuit college of St. Salvator where he matriculated. He received an extensive classical education, which was rounded off with two years of tuition in logic and physics.

His musical talents were soon recognised. He was a choirboy at St. Ulrich and at the Holy Cross. At the Jesuit college he took part in musical plays and won praise for his singing of difficult rôles. He learned the violin and the piano. He watched Italian opera and the musical plays of the Meistersinger Guild. As a boy his mind was moulded by good teachers and by the rich artistic life around him.

In 1737, a year after his father's death, he left the Jesuit college. His father had made plans for him to go into the Church, but instead he went to Salzburg to study philosophy and law at the Benedictine monastery, an unusual course for the son of a craftsman to take. He was then eighteen years old.

All his life he kept his connection with his home town, and took care not to lose his citizenship there. He obtained the consent of the Augsburg town council for his marriage in Salzburg and his children, born in Salzburg, were registered as citizens of Augsburg.

Years later he complained in a letter to an old friend, Johann Jacob Lotter, the music publisher in Augsburg, 'Why can't people who love each other always be together? Must one always look for one's best friends far away?'

The Imperial City of Augsburg

Prospect unser lieben Frauen Thor in Augsburg.
Vuë de la Porte de notre Dame à Augsbourg.

The Frauentorstrasse, where Mozart's father was born

The old workhouse in Augsburg

The house
where
Leopold Mozart
was born

Leopold Mozart was captivated by the artistic life of Salzburg. The architects Fischer von Erlach, Lukas von Hildebrandt and other masters of the Baroque had left their mark. The first opera to be performed in German speaking countries was staged here in a natural setting amongst the rocks. Theatre and music — for Court occasions and the Church — had always been home in the town. There were composers like The Monk of Salzburg, Paul Hofhaymer and Georg Muffat.

The poet Hugo von Hofmannsthal wrote: 'The country of Salzburg is the heart of the heart of Europe. It is situated half-way between Switzerland and the Slav countries, half-way between northern Germany and Lombardy; it lies midway between North and South, between mountains and plains, between the heroic and the idyllic; in its architecture, it lies between town and country, between the ancient and the modern, the Baroque and princely, and the charmingly rustic: Mozart's work is the exact expression of all this. In Central Europe there is no place more beautiful, and it is here that Mozart had to be born.'

A year after taking up his studies in Salzburg Leopold was publicly commended for his special diligence. On the 22 July 1738 he was made a bachelor of Philosophy. A year later, in September 1739, it was recorded in the documents of the university that he was barred from his studies for being absent too often. Only his musical talent saved him from having to return to Augsburg. Count Thurn-Valsassina and Taxis took the expelled student into his service as valet and musician. Leopold dedicated his first compositions to his new master. He engraved the music himself for two violins and bass.

Anna Maria Pertl, who was to be his wife, came from Lake Wolfgang, a few hours journey from Salzburg. She was born on 25 December 1720, the last of three children. Her father, Wolf Niklas Pertl, was the first in his family to have entered the professional classes. There were coachmen and clothmakers among his forbears, but he had studied law in Salzburg and earned his first money as a musician. Later he became deputy prefect of the village of St. Gilgen. A prefect was the highest officer of the law. During his term of office he presided over a court whose jurisdiction covered the two villages of Hüttenstein and St. Gilgen. He died when Anna Maria was four years old. Her mother moved to Salzburg with the children.

Anna Maria was almost the same age as Leopold. No one knows when they first met, but some years before their marriage he had become established as a professional musician. He had written two Passion cantatas for the Episcopal Court and, in 1743, had entered into the service of the Prince Archbishop and become fourth violinist in his orchestra.

The young people were married on 21 November 1747, and were said to be 'the handsomest couple in Salzburg'. They were taken up in a friendly way by the music-lover and rich merchant Lorenz Hagenauer and moved into an apartment on the third floor of his house at No. 9 Getreidegasse.

Later Leopold was to remind his wife in a letter from Milan:

'Today is the anniversary of our wedding day. It was twenty-five years ago, I think, that we had the sensible idea of getting married, one which we had cherished, it is true, for many years. All good things take time!'

Johann Georg Leopold Mozart
b. 14. 11. 1719 in Augsburg
d. 28. 5. 1787 in Salzburg

Anna Maria Walburga Pertl
b. 25. 12. 1720 in St. Gilgen
d. 3. 7. 1778 in Paris

m. 21. 11. 1747
in Salzburg

Johann Leopold Joachim
b. 18. 8. 1748
d. 3. 2. 1749

Maria Anna Cordula
b. 18. 6. 1749
d. 24. 6. 1749

Maria Anna Nepomucena Walburga
b. 13. 5. 1750
d. 29. 7. 1750

Maria Anna Walburga Ignatia ('Nannerl')
b. 30. 7. 1751
d. 29. 10. 1829

Johannes Carolus Amadeus
b. 4. 11. 1752
d. 2. 2. 1753

Maria Crescentia Franziska
b. 9. 5. 1754
d. 27. 6. 1754

Johannes Chrysostomus Wolfgang Theophilus (Amadeus)
b. 27. 1. 1756
d. 5. 12. 1791

Salzburg

15

CONVENIT IGITUR---IN GESTU NEC
VENUSTATEM CONSPICUAM, NEC TURPITU-
-DINEM ESSE, NE AUT HISTRIONES
AUT OPERARII VIDEAMUR ESSE. *Cicer. Rhet. ad H.*
Lib. 3. XV.

G. Eichler delin.   *Jac. Andr. Fridrich Sc. A. V.*

16

Johann Baptist,
Count Thurn-Valsassina and Taxis

The title page of Leopold Mozart's
first composition

SONATE SEI
per Chiesa e da Camera
A TRE
Due Violini
e
Basso.

Dedicate
All Illustrissimo e Reverendissimo
Signore Sign.
Giovani Battista del sacro Romano
impero Conte della Torre, Valsassina
e Tassis Canonico Capitolare della
Metropolitana di Salisburgo e Presi-
dente del Rever.mo Concistoro &c.

Da
LEOPOLDO MOZART.

Salisburgo
Stampate à spese dell' Autore.

Leopold Mozart, 1756

St. Gilgen on Lake Wolfgang

The house where Mozart's mother was born

Hagenauer's house from the rear. Today as in
Mozart's time, there is a street market here

On the third floor of No. 9 Getreidegasse there was always music, day in, day out. One of Leopold Mozart's duties was to teach the violin to the cathedral choirboys. He also became a dealer and sold harpsichords and clavichords built by Friederici in Gera in Thuringia.

But above all he was the teacher of his two children. Nannerl developed into an outstanding pianist. Wolfgang showed, from the beginning, a disturbing talent in every aspect of music, as can be seen from notes made by his father.

In the music-book which Leopold had arranged for Nannerl to practise from, we find remarks in his handwriting. He had put them on the margin of several pieces.

'Little Wolfgang learned the eight minuets above in his fourth year.'

'Little Wolfgang also learned this minuet when he was four years of age.'

'Little Wolfgang learned this piece on 24 January 1761, three days before his fifth birthday, in the evening, between nine o'clock and half past nine o'clock.'

'Little Wolfgang learned this trio and minuet on 26 January 1761, one day before his fifth birthday, at half past nine at night in half an hour.'

'Little Wolfgang's Compositions in the first three months after his fifth birthday.' [These words written by his father on the margin of a sheet of music are the first evidence of Wolfgang Amadeus as a composer.]

His name first appeared in print in the autumn of that year on the programme of a school play, 'Sigismundus Hungariae Rex'. It was performed in the great theatre of the university on 1 and 2 September 1761, to mark the end of the academic year. Some members of the cast were teachers, some were undergraduates. Wolfgang, at the age of five, was by far the youngest and his name comes last on the list of performers — Wolfgangus Mozhart.

In 1756 Leopold Mozart had published a work which made his name famous in the world of music. His *Violin Method* made a stir throughout Europe and gradually appeared in eight languages. The *Historische-Kritische Beiträge zur Aufnahme der Musik* says:

A work of this kind has long been wished for, but one had hardly dared to expect it. Those who are most adept at wielding the bow are not always in control of the pen, and the few who possess equal facility in both often lack the will to write. How much the greater, then, is our obligation towards the author of the present work. The thorough and accomplished virtuoso, the reasonable and methodical teacher, the learned musician — these characteristics, each of which alone makes a man of merit, are all here revealed in one. We may congratulate lovers of this instrument on now having the opportunity of making greater progress at little expense than might otherwise be achieved at great cost in the course of many years.

There is no doubt that Leopold was a sound and reliable teacher for his children. Even though he was often strict and pedantic they loved him dearly. 'Papa comes next after God', Wolfgang used to say.

As to Leopold's character opinions differ. Some blame him for egoism and ambition. Others praise him for patience and kindly good sense. Later, he was to write to his grown-up son: 'You ought to look at me more as an honest friend than a strict father. Try to think whether I have not always treated you in a friendly way and served you as a servant his master.'

Andreas Schachtner, a musician, poet and friend of the family from the beginning, tells us about Wolfgang's childhood. In 1792 — a year after Mozart's death — he wrote to Nannerl:

In answer to your first question: what your late brother's pastimes were in his childhood, apart from his preoccupation with music: This question can have no answer; for no sooner had he begun to busy himself with music than his interest in every other occupation was as dead, and even children's games had to have musical accompaniments if they were to interest him. But before he had began music, he was so ready for any prank spiced with a little humour that he could quite forget food, drink and all things else.

I once went with your father to the house, after Mass on Thursday; we found the four year old Wolfgängerl busy with his pen:

Papa   What are you writing?

Wolfgang   A clavier concerto, the first part is nearly finished.

Papa   Show me.

Wolfgang   It's not ready.

Papa   Show me, it's sure to be interesting.

His father took it from him and showed me a smudge of notes, most of which were written over ink-blots which he had rubbed out. At first we laughed at what seemed such a *galimatias*, but his father then began to observe the most important matter, the notes, the composition; he stared long at the sheet, and then tears, tears of joy and wonder, fell from his eyes. Look, Herr Schachtner, he said, see how correctly and properly it is all written, only it can't be used, for it is so very difficult that no one could play it. Wolfgängerl said: That's why it's a concerto, you must practise it till you get it right.

We played a trio, Papa playing the bass with his viola, Wenzel the first violin, and I the second violin. Wolfgängerl asked to be allowed to play the second violin, but his foolish request was refused, because he had not yet had the least instruction in the violin, and Papa thought that he could not possibly play anything. Wolfgang said: You don't need to have studied in order to play second violin, and when Papa insisted that he should go away and not bother us any more, Wolfgang began to weep bitterly and stamped off with his little violin. I asked them to let him play with me; Papa eventually said: Play with Herr Schachtner, but so softly that we can't hear you, or you will have to go; and so it was. Wolfgang played with me; I soon noticed with astonishment that I was quite superfluous, I quietly put my violin down, and looked at your Papa; tears of wonder and comfort ran down his cheeks at this scene.

Until he was almost nine he was terribly afraid of the trumpet when it was blown alone without other music. Merely to hold a trumpet in front of him was like aiming a loaded pistol at his heart. Papa wanted to cure him of this childish fear and once told me to blow at him despite his reluctance, but my God! I should not have been persuaded to do it; Wolfgängerl scarcely heard the blaring sound, than he grew pale and began to collapse.

Leopold had once reminded his son:

When you sat at the clavier or were otherwise intent on music, no one dared to have the slightest jest with you. Why, even your expression was so solemn that, observing the early flowering of your talent and your ever grave and thoughtful little face, many discerning people of different countries sadly doubted whether your life would be a long one.

Salzburg Cathedral

The font

. . . where Mozart was christened on 28 January 1756

Mozart's father, Leopold. Anonymous oil painting, c. 1765

Mozart's mother, Anna Maria. Anonymous oil painting, c. 1775

The kitchen

Mozart's birthplace in the Getreidegasse

The main room

The inner courtyard

Mozart's clavichord

The strings and hammers
of his clavichord,
still in use when
Mozart was writing
The Magic Flute
and the Requiem

Mozart's first violin

Title-page of the *Violin Method* by Leopold Mozart, 1756

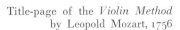

In this room Mozart's cradle is supposed to have stood

Mozart's first composition with comments by his father

Were the talents which Wolfgang so obviously showed to remain hidden in the little town of Salzburg? Leopold knew the times. He knew the value of child-prodigies like Nannerl and Wolfgang. He also knew what had to be done if they were to reap rewards from their talent. Nannerl was then ten years old, Wolfgang not yet six.

He once confessed to his landlord, Lorenz Hagenauer: 'Every moment I lose is lost for ever. And if I ever guessed how precious for youth is time, I realize it now. You know that my children are accustomed to work. But if with the excuse that one thing prevents another they were to accustom themselves to idleness, my whole plan would crumble to pieces.'

The nearest princely residence to Salzburg was at Munich. This is where Leopold took the two children during carnival time in 1762 to present them to the Bavarian Elector Maximilian Joseph III. Their stay lasted three weeks. It was a success and induced Leopold to risk a second journey. This time his goal was Vienna.

In the autumn of the same year the Mozart family left their home town again and this time the mother went as well. Their journey on the Danube — they travelled by post-boat — took more than ten days and their hired carriage went with them on the boat. During the whole of the long journey to Vienna, Leopold never missed an opportunity to let his children perform. Posterity has tried to accuse him of greed and vanity but the question remains of how Wolfgang's genius would have developed without the care and strictness of his father.

Leopold's highest hope was to gain an audience with the Empress Maria Theresa, who, from her throne in Vienna, ruled over countries stretching from Naples to the North Sea. To be allowed to perform at her court meant a de-cisive step forward for Leopold in his ambitious plans.

On 6 October at three o'clock in the afternoon the family arrived in Vienna.

On 8 October the children gave their first concert in the palace of Count Collalto.

On 10 October Countess Sinzendorf took them to the house of Count Wilczek.

On 11 October they performed before the Vice-Chancellor of the Realm, Prince Colloredo-Melz and Wallsee.

And then on 13 October came the fulfilment of Leopold's hope. The family spent the afternoon at Schönbrunn Palace, and the concert was attended by the Empress, her consort the Emperor Francis I, the Archduchess Maria Antoinette and the composer Wagenseil, teacher of the Imperial family.

The same evening the children were presented to Prince Saxe-Hildburg-hausen.

On 14 October the family visited Countess Kinsky.

On 15 October there were three visits on their programme, and the children were presented with gala dress by the Imperial family, who sent their pay-master Mayr to deliver it.

On 16 October the Mozarts visited the young archdukes Ferdinand and Maximilian in the afternoon, and Count Pálffy, the Hungarian Chancellor, in the evening.

On 17 October there was a concert at Count Thurn's [or Thun's]. Count Zinzendorf remarked on it in his diary. 'The little child from Salzburg and his sister played the harpsichord. The poor little fellow plays marvellously, he is a Child of Spirit, lively, charming. His sister's playing is masterly, and he applauded her. Mlle de Gudenus, who plays the harpsichord well, gave him a kiss, and he wiped his face'.

On 21 October the Empress received the Mozart family at Schönbrunn again and on that same evening Wolfgang fell ill. He had given thirteen concerts within a fortnight; it had been too much. He had a high temperature and developed a rash. It was thought to be scarlet fever and he had to stay in bed for ten days and was not allowed out of the house for another four. Some doctors today believe there is a connection between this early serious illness and the later kidney troubles which were supposed to have caused Mozart's death.

On 5 November the children performed at the house of Dr. von Bernhard in gratitude for his treatment.

On 9 November there followed a concert at the house of the Chancellor of the Realm, Count Windischgrätz.

On 19 November the Empress sent the family a present of a hundred ducats. In the afternoon the children performed before the French Ambassador, who issued an invitation for them to come to Versailles. To be invited to the most illustrious court in Europe was for Leopold of the utmost importance.

Except for a journey to play in the old city of Pressburg in the Hungarian part of the Empire, they remained in Vienna giving concerts until the end of the year.

On 5 January 1763, when the Mozart family arrived back in Salzburg, Leopold proudly showed his friends a poetic tribute to his son, 'the little six-year-old clavier player from Salzburg'.

> Child, worthy of our regard, whose ready skill we praise,
> Who, small in stature, like the greatest plays;
> For thee the art of sound will hold no pain,
> Full soon wilt thou to mastery attain.
> . . . and so on.

Lorenz Hagenauer, their landlord, had contributed money towards the cost of the journey to Vienna, and Leopold sent him detailed accounts of all their adventures:

Now we have already been here five days and do not yet know where the sun rises in Vienna, for to this very hour it has done nothing but rain and, with constant wind, has snowed a little now and then, so that we have even seen some snow on the roofs.

One thing I must make a point of telling you, which is, that we quickly got through the local customs and were let off the chief customs altogether. And for this we have to thank our Master Wolferl. For he made friends at once with the customs officer, showed him his clavier, invited him to visit us and played him a minuet on his little fiddle. Thus we got through. The customs officer asked most politely to be allowed to visit us and for this purpose made a note of our lodgings.

Countess Sinzendorf is using her influence on our behalf, and all the ladies are in love with my boy. We are already being talked of everywhere; and when on the 10th I was alone at the opera, I heard the Archduke Leopold from his box say a number of things to another box, namely, that there was a boy in Vienna who played the clavier most excellently.

Everyone is amazed, especially at the boy, and everyone whom I have heard says that his genius is incomprehensible.

Now all that I have time for is to say in great haste that Their Majesties received us with such extraordinary graciousness that, when I shall tell of it, people will declare that I have made it up. Suffice it to say that Wolferl jumped up on the Empress's lap, put his arms round her neck and kissed her heartily. In short, we were there from three to six o'clock and the Emperor himself came out of the next room and made me go in there to hear the Infanta play the violin.

This morning I was summoned to the Privy Paymaster, who received me with the greatest courtesy. His Majesty the Emperor wanted to know whether I could not remain in Vienna a little longer. From whatever point of view I consider it, I foresee that we shall hardly be home before Advent.

Tomorrow we are invited to Count Harrach's from four to six, but which Count Harrach he is I do not know. I shall see where the carriage takes us to. For on every occasion we are fetched by a servant in the nobleman's carriage and are brought home again.

The nobles send us their invitations four, five, six to eight days in advance, in order not to miss us. For instance, the Chief Postmaster, Count Paar, has already engaged us for next Monday. Wolferl now gets enough driving, as he goes out at least twice a day.

Once we drove out at half past two to a place where we stayed until a quarter to four. Count Hardek then fetched us in his carriage and we drove in full gallop to a lady, at whose house we remained till half past five. Thence Count Kaunitz sent to fetch us and we stayed with him until about nine.

I was beginning to think that for fourteen days in succession we were far too happy. God has sent us a small cross and we must thank his infinite goodness that things have turned out as they have. At seven o'clock in the evening of the 21st we again went to the Empress. Our Wolferl, however, was not quite as well as usual and before we drove there and also as he was going to bed, he complained a good deal of his backside and his hips. When he got into bed I examined the places where he said he had pain and found a few spots as large as a kreutzer, very red and slightly raised and painful to the touch.

Thank God, we are well, but we must wait patiently until we can direct our enterprise into its old successful path. For in Vienna the nobility are afraid of pockmarks and all kinds of rash. So my boy's illness has meant a setback of about four weeks. For although since his recovery we have taken in twenty-one ducats, this is a mere trifle, seeing that we only just manage every day on one ducat, and that daily there are additional expenses.

For at least three weeks we have been worried to death with invitations to go to Pressburg after the Feast of the Immaculate Conception. And these became more pressing when we met the greatest nobles of Hungary at the public banquet on the Emperor's birthday. So tomorrow we are off to Pressburg. But I have not the slightest intention of staying there for more than a week.

Homo proponit, Deus disponit. On the 20th I intended to leave Pressburg and on the 26th to take our departure from Vienna in order to reach Salzburg on New Year's Eve. But on the 19th I had unusually bad toothache. During the night my whole face swelled up and on the following day I really looked like a trumpeting angel; so much so that Lieutenant Winkler, the court drummer's brother, who called on us, did not recognise me when he entered the room and thought he had lost his way. In this sad circumstance

I had to console myself with the thought that in any case we were held up by the extraordinarily fierce cold weather which had suddenly come; for the pontoon was removed and it was as much as they could do to get the postbags across the Danube by means of small boats. Hence I had to wait for news that the March (which is not a wide river) was frozen.

Immediately after our return to Vienna our landlady told me that Countess Leopold Kinsky had daily inquired as to whether we had arrived. I called on her on Christmas Day and she said she had waited most anxiously for our return and had postponed a banquet which she wanted to give to Field-Marshal Daun, who would like to make our acquaintance. This banquet she therefore gave on Monday.

Meanwhile I trust that we shall find one another in good health on January 5th. I am looking forward most ardently to telling you a host of things and to reminding you

that I am ever your true friend
Mozart

Munich

The Elector's residence

Vienna

The Empress Maria Theresa and Francis I with their children

Wolfgang in gala dress. Anonymous oil painting, 1763

Maria Anna, called Nannerl. Anonymous oil painting, 1763

In the *Augsburgischer Intelligenz-Zettel*, a newspaper published in Leopold's home town, we find on 19 May 1763, under the heading 'Curiosities', an account of the concerts given by Nannerl and Wolfgang in Vienna.

Just imagine a girl eleven years of age who can perform on the harpsichord or the fortepiano the most difficult sonatas and concertos by the greatest masters, most accurately, readily and with an almost incredible ease, in the very best of taste. This alone cannot fail to fill many with astonishment.

But we fall into utter amazement on seeing a boy aged six at the clavier and hear him, not by any means toy with sonatas, trios and concertos, but play in a manly way, and improvise moreover for hours on end out of his own head, now cantabile, now in chords, producing the best of ideas according to the taste of to-day; and even accompany at sight symphonies, arias and recitatives at the great concerts. — Tell me, does not this exceed all imagination? — And yet it is the simple truth! What is more, I saw them cover the keyboard with a handkerchief, and he plays just as well on this cloth as though he could see the keys.

Now Leopold prepared for the journey to Paris. The Archbishop granted him leave of absence and wished him well. A carriage was procured, a servant engaged and on 9 June 1763 the family set out. They were to be away for three years and their route was to be decided by the location of the princely residences and the possibilities of appearing in large cities.

In Munich Wolfgang performed on the piano and the violin before the Elector Maximilian Joseph III.

In Augsburg the children gave three public concerts.

In Ulm Cathedral Wolfgang played on the big organ.

At the palace of Schwetzingen the children appeared before Karl-Theodor, the Elector-Palatine.

In Heidelberg Wolfgang played the organ in the Church of the Holy Ghost.

In Mainz Nannerl and Wolfgang gave a concert in the 'Römischer König' Inn, where the main room was used as a theatre.

In Frankfurt Leopold advertised his children in the newspaper.

Lovers of music are herewith apprised that a concert will be held at which two children, namely a girl of twelve and a boy of six, will be heard to play with incredible dexterity concertos, trios and sonatas, and then the boy also the same on the violin.

Further be it known that this will be the only concert, since they are immediately afterwards to continue their journey to France and England. Admission: a small thaler per person.

Goethe's father, the Imperial Councillor Johann Caspar Goethe, conscientiously noted in his diary '4 florin, 7 kreutzer for the musical concert of two children'. And Goethe recalled the occasion when he was a very old man 'I myself was about fourteen years old and I remember the little fellow with his wig and sword quite vividly.'

The journey continued via Koblenz, Bonn, Cologne, Aachen, Liège to Brussels, where they stayed for more than a month. Here the children performed before the Governor-General of the Austrian Netherlands, a brother of the Emperor.

On 17 November 1763, the family arrived in Paris. Their stay lasted for four months. In the middle of the century Paris, with more than half a million inhabitants, was three times as large as Vienna. It was a centre for all those who counted or wanted to count in the world of science, literature and art. The Royal Court, with all its splendour and magnificence, was the prototype of all those courts that Leopold Mozart and his family had got to know during their five month journey.

Paris was waiting for the child-prodigies from Salzburg. The *Correspondance Littéraire* described their accomplishments as simply 'unbelievable'. The family moved into the Rue St.-Antoine as guests of the Bavarian Ambassador, Count van Eyck, whose wife was a native of Salzburg. Leopold wrote home to his friend and landlord Lorenz Hagenauer:

> The house where we are staying is so well arranged that everything, even the smallest corner, serves our comfort. We have the Countess's harpsichord in our room. It is a good one, and like ours has two manuals.

Now Leopold had to seek for recommendations, follow up introductions, wait in antechambers. Friedrich Melchior, Baron von Grimm, secretary to the Duc d'Orléans and friend of Diderot and Rousseau, became his most important advocate. But time passed and money was rapidly spent. Leopold kept accounts in his diary. At last everything was arranged. On 24 December he went with his family for two weeks to Versailles. Louis XV, his Queen, the Dauphin, Madame de Pompadour and all the court lavished favours on their guests from Salzburg.

> Yesterday my boy got a gold snuff-box from Madame la Comtesse de Tessé and today my girl was given a small, transparent snuff-box, inlaid with gold, from the Princess Carignan, and Wolfgang a pocket writing case in silver, with silver pens with which to write his compositions; it is so small and exquisitely made that it is impossible to describe it. My children have taken almost everyone by storm.

On New Year's Day 1764 the Mozarts were invited to attend at the royal table, an exceptional privilege. Leopold proudly described the occasion:

What appeared most extraordinary to these French people was that at the grand-couvert on the evening of New Year's Day, not only was it neccessary to make room for us all to go up to the royal table, but my Wolfgang was graciously privileged to stand beside the Queen the whole time, to talk constantly to her, entertain her and kiss her hands repeatedly, besides partaking of the dishes which she handed him from the table. The Queen speaks as good German as we do and, as the King knows none, she interpreted to him everything that our gallant Wolfgang said.

At his own expense Leopold now published the first works of his son — sonatas for harpsichord with violin accompaniment. Opus 1 is dedicated to the Princesse Victoire, the second daughter of the King, Opus 2 to the Comtesse de Tessé, who had been so generous to Wolfgang. Leopold was well aware of the effect these publications were to have:

Picture yourself the furore which they will make in the world when people read on the title page that they have been composed by a seven-year-old child; and when the sceptics are challenged to test him, as he already has been, imagine the sensation when he asks someone to write down a minuet or some tune or other and then immediately and without touching the clavier writes in the bass and, if it is wanted, the second violin part. In due course you will hear how fine these sonatas are.

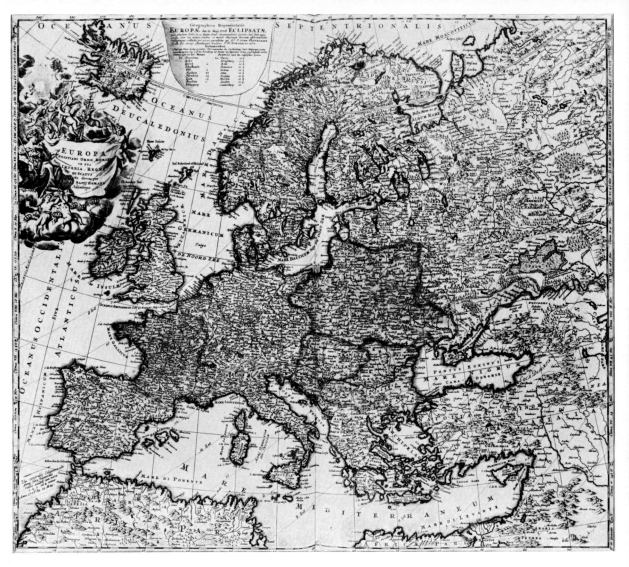

Europe in Mozart's time

Paris.

A page from Nannerl's travel diary

Friedrich Melchior von Grimm

The Hôtel de Beauvais in Paris where the Mozart family stayed

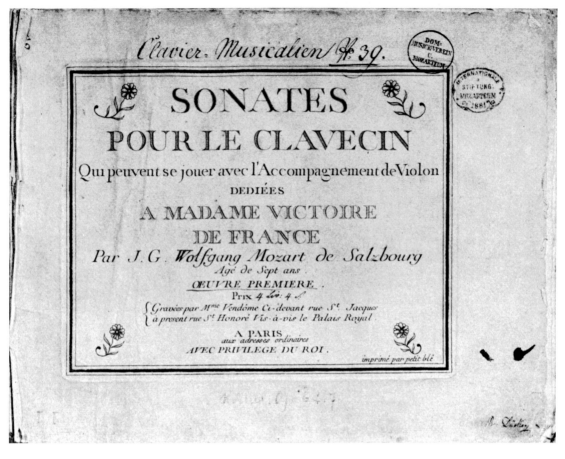

Mozart's first published work

King Louis XV and his wife Marie Leszczynska
(*Above*) Versailles

Leopold Mozart with Wolfgang and Nannerl. Engraving by Jean Baptist Delafosse, 1764

On 10 April the family set off for England, leaving their carriage in Calais. Nannerl wrote in her diary 'At Calais I saw how the sea runs away and then swells up again.'

Leopold described the crossing to Lorenz Hagenauer, ironically referring to the Channel as the Maxglanerbach, a tiny stream in Salzburg. 'Thank God we have safely crossed the Maxglanerbach. Yet we have not done so without making a heavy contribution in vomiting. I, however, had the worst time of it.' And he continued 'Whoever has too much money should just make a journey from Paris to London, for his purse will certainly be lightened'.

On 23 April the Mozarts arrived in London. Their fame had preceded them and only four days later, on the 27th, they were received at Court, where Wolfgang and Nannerl gave a performance before King George III and Queen Charlotte. Leopold received a fee of twenty-four guineas for this.

> The present was only twenty-four guineas which we received immediately on leaving the King's apartment, but the graciousness with which both His Majesty the King and Her Majesty the Queen received us cannot be described. In short their easy manner and friendly ways made us forget they were the King and Queen of England. At all courts up to the present we have been received with extraordinary courtesy. But the welcome which we have been given here exceeds all others. A week later we were walking in St. James's Park. The King came along driving with the Queen and, although we all had on different clothes, they recognised us nevertheless and not only greeted us, but the King opened the window, leaned out and saluted us, especially our Master Wolfgang, nodding to us and waving his hand.

As a special honour, the children were invited to take part in two concerts for the benefit of Carlo Graziani, the cellist and composer, and then on 19 May they appeared again at court. At this second Royal Command performance Wolfgang played the piano as before and also the organ.

> The King placed before him not only works by Wagenseil, but of Bach, Abel and Handel, and he played off everything prima vista. He played so splendidly on the King's organ that they all value his organ-playing more highly than his clavier-playing. Then he accompanied the Queen in an aria which she sang, and also a flautist who played a solo. Finally he took the bass part of some airs of Handel (which happened to be lying there) and played the most beautiful melody on it and in such a manner that everyone was amazed. In short, what he knew when we left Salzburg is a mere shadow compared with what he knows now.

Leopold now arranged a public concert for the benefit of Nannerl and Wolfgang. He fixed the date for 5 June, the day the King's birthday was celebrated in London, and for which many members of the nobility were expected to be in town. He himself drafted the announcements which appeared four times in the *Public Advertiser*.

> *For the Benefit of Miss Mozart of Eleven, and Master Mozart of Seven Years of Age, Prodigies of Nature.*
>
> *The greatest Prodigy that Europe or that even Human Nature has to boast of.*
>
> *It surpasses all Understanding or all Imagination.*
>
> *Ticket at Half a Guinea each, to be had of Mr. Mozart, at Mr. Couzin's, Hair-Cutter, in Cecil-Court, St. Martin's Lane.*

In his account to his friend in Salzburg Leopold dwelt mostly on the difficulties of the arrangements.

> We had a week, or rather two or three days only, in which to distribute the 'billets', for before that date there was hardly anyone in London. But although for this kind of concert four to eight weeks are usually necessary for the distribution of the 'billets', which here they call 'tickets', to the amazement of everyone there were present a couple of hundred persons, including all the leading people in London, and everyone was delighted. I cannot say whether I shall have a profit of one hundred guineas, as I have not yet received the money for thirty-six tickets for my lord March and forty tickets from a friend in town and from various others; and the expenses are surprisingly great. The hall without lighting and music-stands costs five guineas. Each clavier, of which I have had two on account of the concerto for two claviers, costs half a guinea. The first violin gets three guineas and so on; and all who play the solos and concertos three, four and five guineas. The ordinary players receive half a guineas and so forth. But, fortunately for me, all the musicians as well as the hall and everything else only cost me twenty guineas, because most of the performers would not accept anything. Well, God be praised, that is over and we have made something.

Certainly the evening was a success. As soon as it was over invitations were showered on Leopold from all directions. He considered journeys to Germany and Scandinavia, even to Russia. But a month later he fell seriously ill. The family moved to Chelsea, which was then a village outside London famous for its healthy situation.

So that you may know how my illness started, I must tell you that in England there is a kind of native complaint, which is called a 'cold'. That is why you hardly ever see people wearing summer clothes. They all wear cloth garments. This so-called 'cold' in the case of people who are not constitutionally sound, becomes so dangerous that in many cases it develops into a 'consumption' as they call it here; but I call it 'febrem lentem'.

The Mozart family remained in Chelsea until the autumn and the earnings from the concerts were soon spent. On 25 October the children were again received at Court. Leopold arranged for the engraving and printing of Wolfgang's Opus 3, six sonatas for the piano, with optional accompaniment for the violin or flute. These he dedicated to the Queen. Yet the great and general interest in the 'marvel of nature' had faded and although he had advertised a public concert five times, it was not as well attended as he had hoped. In a letter to Salzburg he aired his grievances:

I know what the reason is, and why we are not treated more generously, although since our arrival in London we have made a few hundred guineas. I did not accept a proposal which was made to me. But what is the use of saying much about a matter upon which I have decided deliberately after mature consideration and several sleepless nights and which is now done with, as I will not bring up my children in such a dangerous place (where the majority of the inhabitants have no religion and where one only has evil examples before one). You would be amazed if you saw the way children are brought up here: not to mention other matters connected with religion.

An important document of this time is a report to the Royal Society by Daines Barrington. In it Barrington describes how he tested 'little Mozart'.

I carried with me a manuscript duet, which was composed by an English gentleman to some favourite words in Metastasio's opera of *Demofoonte*. My intention was to have an irrefragable proof of his abilities as a player at sight, it being absolutely impossible that he could have ever seen the music before. The score was no sooner put upon his desk, than be began to play the composition in a most masterly manner, as well as in the time and style which corresponded with the intention of the composer. I mention this circumstance, because the greatest masters often fail in these particulars on the first trial.

I then told his father that I should be glad to hear some of his extempore compositions. The father shook his head at this, saying, that it depended entirely upon his being as it were musically inspired. Happening to know that little Mozart was much taken notice of by Manzoli, the famous singer, who came over to England in 1764, I said to the boy, that I should be glad to hear an extempore 'Love Song', such as his friend Manzoli might choose in an opera. The boy on this (who continued to sit at the harpsichord) looked back with much archness, and immediately began five or six lines of a jargon recitative proper to introduce a love song. He then played a symphony which might correspond with an air composed to the single word 'Affetto'.

Finding that he was in humour, I then desired him to compose a 'Song of Rage'. This lasted also about the same time as the 'Song of Love'; and in the middle of it he had worked himself up to such a pitch that he beat his harpsichord like a person possessed, rising sometimes in his chair. The word he pitched on for this second composition was, 'Perfido'.

Barrington tells us that Wolfgang's technique in piano playing was masterly, that he had a thorough knowledge of composition, that he was a master of modulation, that he also played with a handkerchief covering the keys. Such astonishing talent made Barrington suspect Leopold of cheating about the boy's age. He was only convinced by Wolfgang's childish behaviour.

Whilst he was playing to me, a favourite cat came in, upon which he immediately left his harpsichord, nor could we bring him back for a considerable time. He would also sometimes run about the room with a stick between his legs by way of a horse.

To make quite sure, Barrington obtained an extract from the register in Salzburg which showed that Wolfgang was eight years and five months old. The report then compares him with Handel, who began to play the clavichord when he was seven and to compose when he was nine and points out that Mozart had started much earlier. It goes on to say 'It may be hoped that little Mozart may possibly attain to the same advanced years as Handel.'

For Wolfgang the most important event in London was his meeting with Johann Christian Bach. Johann Christian, the youngest son of Johann Sebastian Bach, was born in Leipzig on 5 September 1735. After his father's death, when he was fifteen, he went to Berlin to be taught by his brother, Philipp Emanuel. Four years later he became Kapellmeister in Milan and was able to continue his studies under Padre Martini in Bologna. He was converted to the Catholic faith and became Cathedral Organist in Milan. He made a name as a composer of operas and went to London in 1762. There he became Wolfgang's patron and teacher. From him Wolfgang learned the elements of Italian opera. His influence can be traced for many years in Mozart's work.

58

London

Johann Christian Bach

Daines Barrington

A View of the Queen's Palace in St. James's Park, taken from a Tree in the Green Park, near the End of the Mall.

The Queen's Palace in London, where the present Buckingham Palace stands

King George III

His wife, Queen Charlotte

The house in Ebury Street
where the Mozarts stayed

Announcement of concert
in the *Public Advertiser*

64

To all Lovers of Sciences.
THE greateſt Prodigy that
Europe, or that even Human Nature has to
boaſt of, is, without Contradiction, the little German
Boy WOLFGANG MOZART; a Boy, Eight Years
old, who has, and indeed very juſtly, raiſed the Ad-
miration not only of the greateſt Men, but alſo of the
greateſt Muſicians in Europe. It is hard to ſay, whether his Execution upon the Harpſichord and his playing and ſinging at Sight, or his own Caprice, Fancy,
and Compoſitions for all Inſtruments, are moſt aſton ſh-
ing. The Father of this Miracle, being obliged by
Deſire of ſeveral Ladies and Gentlemen to poſtpone, for
a very ſhort Time, his Departure from England, will
give an Opportunity to hear this little Compoſer and
his Siſter, whoſe muſical Knowledge wants not Apo-
logy. Performs every Day in the Week, from Twelve
to Three o'Clock in the Great Room, at the Swan and
Hoop, Cornhil. Admittance 2s. 6d. each Perſon,
The two Children will play alſo together with four
Hands upon the ſame Harpſichord, and put upon it a
Handkerchief, without ſeeing the Keys.

On 1 August 1765, after a stay of fifteen months, the Mozart family left England to continue their journey through Europe. At Calais they picked up their carriage and travelled via Dunkirk to Lille. They had to spend a whole month in Lille, because Wolfgang fell ill, and then they travelled on through Ghent, Antwerp and Rotterdam to The Hague.

There Nannerl fell ill. The first concerts at court — before Princess Caroline of Nassau-Weilburg — had to be given without her. Her illness, intestinal typhoid, was so serious that on the 21 October she received Extreme Unction. As soon as she recovered Wolfgang caught the same disease and for over two months his life too was in danger.

My daughter was scarcely a week out of bed and had just begun to walk across the bedroom floor by herself, when on November 15th little Wolfgang contracted an illness which in four weeks has made him so wretched that he is not only absolutely unrecognisable, but has nothing left but his tender skin and his little bones and for the last five days has been carried daily from his bed to a chair. Yesterday and today, however, we led him a few times across the room so that gradually he may learn to use his feet and stand upright by himself. You would like to know what was wrong with him? God knows! I am tired of describing illnesses to you.

It was not until January 1766 that the children were able to appear again together, first at a public concert in The Hague and then in Amsterdam. In March they set off once more. Their father tried to speed up the journey, yet he did not want to give up any chance of success. There were still great houses and large cities which clamoured for the children. In the drawing-rooms of Europe everybody talked about them. The newspapers spread their fame and Wolfgang was compared to Orpheus.

They went to Haarlem, back to Amsterdam, and on through Brussels, Paris, Dijon, Lyon to Geneva. They spent the autumn in Switzerland, visiting Lausanne, Berne and Zurich, travelled on via Munich, where the children performed again at the court of the Bavarian Elector, and arrived back in Salzburg on 29 November 1766. They had left the town in June of 1763.

On the day of their homecoming, Father Beda Hübner, the librarian of the monastery of St. Peter in Salzburg, wrote in his diary:

The boy, Wolfgangerl, has not grown very much during this journey, but Nannerl has become tolerably tall and almost marriageable already. There is a strong rumour that the Mozart family will again not long remain here, but will soon visit the whole of Scandinavia and the whole of Russia, and perhaps even travel to China. De facto, I believe it to be certain that nobody is more celebrated in Europe than Herr Mozart with his two children.

On 8 November Hübner wrote:

This very day I found myself, quite unexpectedly, at the Mozart family's, where to my utmost and particular delight I not only heard the harpsichord, or clavier, played by the boy Wolfgangerl, but also saw with my eyes and touched with my hands all the presents and tributes Herr Mozart and his children have received from great monarchs and princes during their journey. Of gold pocket watches he has brought home nine. Of gold snuff-boxes he has received twelve. Of gold rings set with the most handsome precious stones he has so many that he does not know himself how many; ear-rings for the girl, necklaces, knives with golden blades, bottle-holders, writing-tackle, toothpick boxes, gold objects for the girl, writing-tablets and suchlike gewgaws without number and without end. It is just like inspecting a church treasury, not perhaps because of its value, but because of its rarity, for so many things from various countries are rarely to be seen collected together. In addition Herr Mozart had bought very many things cheaply in these foreign countries, which he will sell here at a high price, and in this way make a lot of money on the spot! For this Herr Mozart has such a clever, incentive, energetic and sensible head that I am sure there are few who would have thought all this out and managed it as Herr Mozart has done.

During his three years of travel between the age of seven and ten, Wolfgang had composed a number of works, among others:

In Paris, four sonatas for piano with various accompaniments,

In London, six similar sonatas, two symphonies and one motet 'God is our Refuge'.

In The Hague, six sonatas for piano and violin, some variations for the piano and the instrumental quodlibet 'Galimathias musicum'.

Now the everyday life of Salzburg began for them again, but here too Wolfgang was kept hard at work playing and composing for the great people of the town, for the Archbishop's Court, for the cathedral and the university.

An oratorio, 'Die Schuldigkeit des ersten Gebots', of which he composed the first act, was performed on 12 March 1767, in the Rittersaal in the Archbishop's palace. The composers of the other acts were Michael Haydn, the brother of Joseph Haydn, and Cajetan Adlgasser, the court organist.

He played at a banquet in honour of the Spanish Ambassador.

In Holy Week on 17 April his passion music was heard in Salzburg Cathedral.

He wrote the music for the Latin school play *Apollo and Hyacinth*.

But at least there was a rest from travel, a short one as it turned out, because after only ten months at home Leopold prepared for another journey to Vienna. Great festivities were to take place there at the marriage of the Archduchess

Maria Josepha to King Ferdinand IV of Naples and he saw another opportunity of presenting his children.

On 15 September 1767 the family arrived in the capital. But the wedding did not take place. A disastrous epidemic of smallpox broke out and the bride-to-be was one of those who died. The Mozart family fled to Olmütz, but neither of the children escaped the illness. First Wolfgang fell sick and then Nannerl. They were unable to return to Vienna till January of the next year and then, at last, they were received at Court. But it was a very different court from the one they had known six years earlier. The Emperor Francis I had died in 1765 and the Empress Maria Theresa lived a retired life. The new Emperor, her son, Joseph II, according to Leopold 'positively abhorred everything that might entail any expenditure'. And the nobility followed suit.

Wolfgang, now twelve, could no longer cause a sensation as a child-prodigy. The Viennese musicians regarded him as a rival. The Emperor suggested that he should write an opera for the Imperial Theatre, and he composed *La Finta Semplice*, based on a comedy by Goldoni, but it was not put on. There was an intrigue against it led by the impressario of the theatre, Giuseppe Affligio, an unscrupulous character whose crimes later resulted in his ending his life as a galley slave. Leopold appealed to the Emperor:

> The opera had now been ready for some weeks. They began to copy it; and the first act was distributed to the singers, with the second following immediately. The rehearsals were about to begin; only — how was I to suspect such a thing? — this was where the persecutions of my son also began.
>
> A few days later I heard that Affligio had decided not to give the boy's opera at the theatre at all. Wishing to know the true state of affairs, I called on him, and received the information that he had called the singers together, and that they confessed that although the opera was composed incomparably well, it was untheatrical and could not be performed by them. I replied that he could not expect the boy to have taken the pains to write an opera for nothing. I reminded him of his agreement. To this my reasonable demand he gave me an incomprehensible answer, which betrayed his embarrassment, until at last he left me with the most shamelessly unkind expressions: if I wished to see my boy prostituted, he would see to it that the opera was laughed to scorn and hissed. Was this, then, to be the reward offered to my son for the great labour of writing an opera? — and last, what of that which I have most at heart, my son's honour and fame?

The Emperor ignored this apeal and the opera was not put on (its first performance took place in Salzburg a year later). But during this visit, Wolfgang wrote a second work for the stage, the one-act singspiel *Bastien und Bastienne*, and this was performed in Vienna at the house of the famous Dr Anton Mesmer.

On 5 January 1769 the Mozart family returned to Salzburg and Leopold resumed his duties at the Episcopal Court. He had been away for sixteen months, a much longer period than the leave of absence the Archbishop had granted him. His pay had therefore been withheld and again he had to draw up a petition:

> Since this stay of mine in Vienna was made against my will and turned out to my disadvantage and to safeguard my and my child's honour I was unable to leave Vienna earlier, I now therefore most humbly address to Your Serene Highness the request that I should not only be paid for the past month, but that you will also be most graciously pleased to give your command that the arrears should also be handed to me.

This resulted in back payments of only two months' salary.

Leopold was not to stay at home for long. He had written to Lorenz Hagenauer from Vienna:

> Should I perhaps sit down in Salzburg with the empty hope of some better fortune, let Wolfgang grow up, and allow myself and my children to be made fools of until I reach the age which prevents me from travelling and until he attains the age and physical appearance which no longer attract admiration for his merits?

Wolfgang playing at Prince Louis-François de Conte's in the Temple. Oil painting by Michel Barthélemy Ollivier, 1766

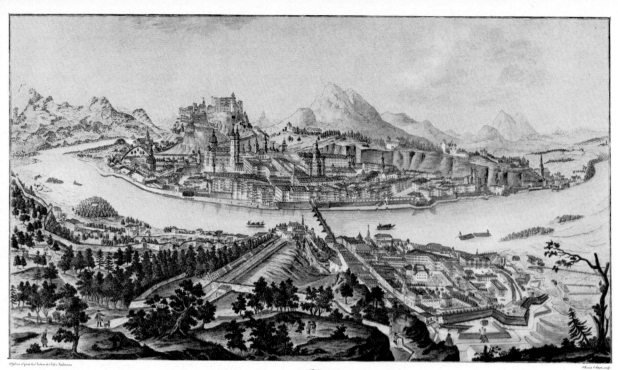

VUE DE LA VILLE CAPITALE DE SALZBOURG AVEC LA FORTERESSE.
Dédié a l'Illustre Chapitre de l'Eglise Metropolitaine de Salzbourg.

Title page of
'Die Schuldigkeit des ersten Gebotes',
performed in Salzburg, 1767

The 'Rittersaal' of the residence of the Prince Archbishop

The Throne-room of the residence of the Prince Archbishop

Leopold had long planned to take Wolfgang to Italy. The Archbishop granted him leave, generously contributing 120 ducats towards the cost of the journey and on 13 December 1769 father and son — accompanied by a servant — set out towards the south. Now for the first time Wolfgang showed himself a letterwriter. The very day after their departure Leopold wrote home to Salzburg and Wolfgang added postscripts to his mother and sister:

Dearest Mamma! My heart is completely enchanted with all these pleasures, because it is so jolly on this journey, because it is so warm in the carriage and because our coachman is a fine fellow who, when the road gives him the slightest chance, drives so fast. Papa will have already described the journey to Mamma. The reason why I am writing to Mamma is to show her that I know my duty and that I am with the deepest respect her devoted son
Wolfgang Mozart

The postscript to Nannerl is in Italian. Even at that age he had a wide knowledge of languages though there is no evidence that he ever went to school. He had learned all he knew from his father, who laid special emphasis on languages — French, Italian, English and Latin. Theory of music, of course, always occupied first place.

On 5 January 1770 he gave his first concert in Italy at the Accademia Filarmonica in Verona. Here on 6 and 7 January, Saverio dalla Rosa painted one of the rare portraits of Wolfgang, commissioned by their friend, the famous patron of music, Pietro Lugiati.

Their next stop was Mantua, where a great concert took place at the Teatro Scientifico 'on the occasion of the arrival of the most highly skilled youth Signor Amadeo Mozart.'

The journey went on via Bozzolo and Cremona to Milan, where they stayed for seven weeks. It was Carnival time and Leopold and Wolfgang took part in the festivities. Whenever possible they went to the theatre to hear Italian opera. They met Piccinni and Sammartini. Wolfgang played on three occasions at Count Firmian's. He also gave a public concert. On 13 March his father was able to write home 'Wolfgang has been asked to write the first opera here for next Christmas'.

They travelled on with a short stop at Parma to Bologna, Europe's oldest university town, a cultural centre and the dwelling place of many artists and scholars. When Wolfgang played before the leading nobles of the town the famous Padre Martini was in the audience.

Giambattista Martini was born on 24 April 1706 in Bologna. As the son of a violinist he received an extensive musical education and in 1721 he entered the Franciscan Order. He is known as a composer of church music and mainly as a scholar and was the highest authority in Italy on all questions of music. 'The fact that Padre Martini, the idol of the Italians, speaks well of Wolfgang' wrote Leopold to his wife, 'has increased his reputation all over Italy.' Padre Martini devoted himself to Wolfgang, worked with him and corrected his compositions. Wolfgang always regarded him as a friend.

On 30 March the travellers reached Florence. It was here that Wolfgang met Thomas Linley, the young English violinist, who was then fourteen.

> The two boys performed one after the other throughout the whole evening, constantly embracing each other. On the following day the little Englishman, a most charming boy, had his violin brought to our rooms and played the whole afternoon, Wolfgang accompanying him on his own.

Leopold and Wolfgang then spent a busy month in Rome, visited Naples and went back to Rome post-haste, taking only twenty-seven hours on the return journey.

> As soon as we got to our bedroom, Wolfgang sat down on a chair and at once began to snore and to sleep so soundly that I completely undressed him and put him to bed without his showing the least sign of waking up. Indeed he went on snoring. When he awoke after nine o'clock in the morning, he did not know where he was.

In a patent dated 4 July 1770 Pope Clement XIV honoured Wolfgang Amadeus Mozart with the title 'Knight of the Golden Spur'. Gluck and Dittersdorf had received this papal order before him, but not with the same high rank, which had hitherto been awarded to only one musician, Orlando di Lasso (d. 1588). On 5 July Cardinal Pallavicini presented Wolfgang with the golden cross on a red sash, the sword and the spurs. Wolfgang now had the right to call himself Knight, but he only once — in high spirits — used his title. On the 8th, the young musician, wearing the insignia of his order, was received by the Pope in audience.

When soon after this the Mozarts made their second visit to Bologna they were almost daily visitors to the house of Padre Martini. Wolfgang was made a member of the Accademia Filarmonica. The minimum age for members is laid down in the statutes of the Academy as twenty — yet, after the usual examination, he was elected at fourteen. His father described the occasion:

> On the 9th he had to appear in the Hall of the Academy at four o'clock in the afternoon. There the Princeps Accademiae and the two Censores, who are all three old Kapellmeisters, put before him, in the presence of all the

members, an antiphon taken out of an antiphoner, which he had to arrange for four parts in the anteroom, into which the Bedellus led him, locking the door behind him. When Wolfgang had finished it, it was examined by the Censores and all the Kapellmeisters and Compositores. Then a vote was taken, which was done by means of white and black balls. As all the balls were white, Wolfgang was called in and all the members clapped their hands as he entered and congratulated him, and the Princeps Accademiae informed him, on behalf of the company, that he had passed the examination.

Then they left for Milan where Wolfgang had to fulfill his contract for the opera. He wrote shortly to his mother:

I cannot write much for my fingers are aching from composing so many recitatives. Mamma, I beg you to pray for me that my opera may go well.

The dress rehearsal took place on 24 December. On the 26th *Mitridate, Re di Ponto* was performed in the ducal castle — the Teatro Regio Ducal — for the first time. There were twenty-two consecutive performances, Wolfgang conducting the first three at the harpsichord. The extraordinary success led to a second commission for Milan: his new opera *Lucio Silla* was to be ready for the carnival in 1773.

The next stops were Turin, Venice and Padua. At Padua he received a commission to compose an oratorio 'La Betulia liberata' to words by Metastasio. And now on their return journey they went on through Vicenza to Verona, where Wolfgang had given his first concert in Italy and where he was now elected honorary Kapellmeister of the Accademia Filarmonica, and then on through Rovereto, and Innsbruck. After almost sixteen months' absence they arrived in Salzburg on 28 March 1771.

They only had a short rest at home. In August they set out once more for Milan, where Wolfgang carried out a commission from the Empress Maria Theresa to compose the 'serenata teatrale' *Ascanio in Alba*. This was to celebrate the marriage of her son, the Archduke Ferdinand, which took place there in October. The libretto was late in arriving from Vienna and Wolfgang had only about four weeks for his work. The first performance took place on 17 October, once more in the Teatro Regio Ducal. Two days later Leopold wrote to his wife 'We are constantly addressed in the street by courtiers and other persons who wish to congratulate Wolfgang'.

Leopold and Wolfgang arrived back in Salzburg on 15 December. On the following day their patron, the Prince Archbishop Sigismund Count Schrattenbach, died. He had always generously helped and promoted the Mozart family.

His interest in music was a friendly, patriarchal one. Hieronymus, Count Colloredo, who succeeded him was a different kind of man, dry and no friend of the Muses. With a bust of Voltaire on his writing desk he belonged entirely to the age of reason and regarded the Arts with suspicion. For him their place was in Court ceremonial where they served his craving for power. Artists, and especially musicians, were to be treated with circumspection, and that applied to the Mozart family. Again Leopold asked for leave of absence. For the third time he and Wolfgang were bound for Italy, and they set out on 24 October 1772.

Lucio Silla, the second opera Wolfgang had been asked to compose for Milan, opened there on Boxing Day and was played twenty-six times during the Carnival. Leopold wrote with satisfaction to his wife 'Thank God, the opera is an extraordinary success, and every day the theatre is surprisingly full. Every evening arias are repeated.'

They did not return to Salzburg until March. Wolfgang Amadeus Mozart was now seventeen years old, rebellious, self-assured, 'in opposition' like all young people of his age. After his travels and experiences the town must have seemed even more cramped to him than it was. The one journey to Italy had turned into three. Altogether father and son had spent almost twenty-five months in the south, travelling about between Naples and Milan. There had been great successes for Wolfgang; honorary Kapellmeister in Verona, member of the Academy in Bologna, knighted in Rome, acclaimed in Milan. Yet he could not make a living in Italy.

Italy gave him much artistically. He learned to write Italian opera, to handle melody and voice with virtuosity, and everything he learned he made his own, transforming and developing it throughout his life — a way that led him towards *Le nozze di Figaro* and *Don Giovanni*.

Before the first Italian journey Archbishop Count Schrattenbach had nominated Wolfgang Concert Master of the Court music, so that he should not present himself abroad without a title. Now Count Colloredo confirmed the appointment and fixed a yearly salary of 150 florins — which is what a clerk earned at the Episcopal court.

The Piazza Navona, Rome

Mozart, Knight of the Golden Spur. Anonymous oil painting, 1777

(*Opposite, top*) St. Peter's, Rome. (*Opposite, below*) Pope Clement XIV, who made Mozart a Knight of the Golden Spur.

San Luca, Bologna

Mozart's certificate of membership of the Accademia Filarmonica in Bologna

The antiphon which Mozart wrote as his examination piece

Padre Giovanni Battista Martini

The Opera House, Milan

Mozart in Verona. Oil painting by Saverio dalla Rosa, January 1770

The Döllerer-Gässchen, a narrow street in Salzburg

The garden of Schloss Mirabell, Salzburg

Sigismund Christoph, Count von Schrattenbach

Hieronymus, Count von Colloredo

In the last three years Wolfgang had not only distinguished himself as a soloist, not only written those three Italian operas and the oratorio. He had composed a number of concert arias, in Lodi he finished his first string quartet and in Bologna, he had spent three months working almost daily with Padre Martini, he had completed a Miserere. During his short spells in Salzburg he had written church sonatas and symphonies. In the few months he spent there between December 1771 and the autumn of 1772 he wrote eight symphonies and four divertimenti. In honour of the new Archbishop he had composed the dramatic serenata *Il sogno di Scipio*. Altogether there were over fifty works.

In February 1772 his father had made an offer to the famous music publishers Breitkopf and Härtel in Leipzig.

> We arrived back from Milan on December 15th. As my son has again won great honour by his composition of the dramatic serenata, he has been asked to write the first opera for the coming carnival in Milan. We shall therefore remain in Salzburg until the end of September and then travel to Italy for the third time. Should you wish to print any of my son's compositions, this intervening period would be the best time to order them. You have only to state what you consider most suitable. He can let you have clavier compositions or trios for two violins and violoncello, or quartets for two violins, viola and violoncello, or symphonies for two violins, viola, two horns, two oboes or transverse flutes, and double bass. In short, my son will write whatever kind of composition you may consider most profitable to yourself, provided you let us know in good time.

There was no answer to this letter.

Presumable in the spring of 1773 the Mozart family moved from the Getreidegasse to the Tanzmeisterhaus — the dancing master's house. Leopold had been planning to move for some time. He had written to his wife from Venice:

> With God's help we shall be back at Salzburg for Easter. I nearly put 'back at home', but then remembered we cannot live there any more. You must write and say whether we can find lodgings at the Stern's or the Saulentzl's. We cannot all sleep together like soldiers any more. Wolfgang is no longer seven years old.

The Tanzmeisterhaus is situated on the right bank of the river Salzach, on the Hannibalplatz which is now known as the Makartplatz. Leopold rented the upper floor — eight rooms. This was to be Wolfgang's home until his twenty-fifth year. The music room — the Tanzmeistersaal — is still in use. The works he wrote there are still played in it as they were when he lived in the house, but the other rooms were destroyed during the Second World War.

After only four months in the Tanzmeisterhaus, Leopold and Wolfgang left Salzburg again. They had been unsuccessful in finding an appointment for Wolfgang in Italy and now they set out for Vienna with renewed hope. However, after their audience with the Empress on 5 August Leopold — once more disappointed — wrote to his wife: 'Her Majesty the Empress was very gracious to us, but that was all. I am saving up a full account until our return, for it is impossible for me to give it in writing'.

On the other hand Wolfgang gained rich experience in music. Joseph Haydn and Gluck, Salieri and Wagenseil, Karl Ditters von Dittersdorf, Albrechtsberger, Hasse — also countless singers and virtuosi made up the musical life of Vienna. The 'young man' Mozart was regarded as one of them. Hardly anyone now remembered the child prodigy.

In Vienna he completed six string quartets, wrote serenades, a divertimento, variations for piano, and worked on the music for the play *Thamos, King of Egypt*. They stayed in Vienna for two months and then went back to Salzburg.

The Tanzmeisterhaus became the centre of an animated social circle. The Mozart family had many friends. Among them were:
The Archbishop's first physician, Silvester Barisani, and his wife Theresia
The merchant Lorenz Hagenauer, their landlord from the Getreidegasse, and his wife Maria Theresia
Sigmund Haffner, son of the mayor of Salzburg, who commissioned the 'Haffner Serenade' for the marriage of his sister with Franz Anton Späth
Luise, the daughter of the iron magnate Georg Joseph Robinig von Rottenfeld
Michael Haydn, first concert-master and composer, brother of Joseph Haydn, who was even then highly esteemed
Maria Anna, Countess Lodron, the wife of the High Chamberlain
Andreas Schachtner, the court trumpeter
Anton Cajetan Adlgasser, the court organist
The Abbé Joseph Bullinger, house chaplain to Count Lodron
Wolf Joseph Count Uiberacker, Councillor at the Exchequer
The District Councillor Joachim von Schiedenhofen, whose diary is full of information about Mozart's life.

On 6 December 1774 Schiedenhofen noted down: 'Herr Mozart travelled to Munich with his son this very day, in order to produce the opera buffa composed by the latter'.

Wolfgang had received a commission from the Bavarian Elector Maximilian Joseph III to write an opera, *La Finta Giardiniera*, for the carnival in Munich. After some delay it had its first performance on 13 January, for which Nannerl too came to Munich. Wolfgang wrote happily to his mother:

Thank God! My opera was performed yesterday, the 13th, for the first time and was such a success that it is impossible for me to describe the applause to Mamma. In the first place, the whole theatre was so packed that a great many people were turned away. Then after each aria there was a terrific noise, clapping of hands and cries of 'Viva Maestro'. Her Highness the Electress and the Dowager Electress (who were sitting opposite me) also called out 'Bravo' to me. After the opera was over and during the pause when there is usually silence until the ballet begins, people kept on clapping all the time and shouting 'Bravo'; now stopping, now beginning again and so on. Afterwards I went off with Papa to a certain room through which the Elector and the whole Court had to pass and I kissed the hands of the Elector and Electress and Their Highnesses, who were all very gracious. Early this morning His Grace the Bishop of Chiemsee sent me a message, congratulating me on the extraordinary success of my opera.

They did not get back to Salzburg till 7 March. Extracts from Schiedenhofen's diary give us glimpses of their life there.

19 April: 'In the evening Councillor Mölck came to me, with whom I went to the Mozart's, where I met the castrato Consoli and the transverseflute player Becke, both from Munich'.
20 April: 'Afterwards I went to Mass and thence to Court, where the Serenade by Mozart was rehearsed. Thence I accompanied the Robinigs home'.
22 April: 'In the evening I went with the Town Syndic to the Serenade at Court'.

And so the days passed in Salzburg.
9 August: 'After dinner to the Final-Musik composed by Herr Mozart. I went to Mirabell first, and then to the University with Herr von Luidl and my sister. The acquaintances I met were the Barisanis, the Loeses and the Robinigs'.
23 August: 'After dinner to the Final-Musik, which was by Mozart. I saw there the Robinigs, Barisanis, Daubrawas and Mozarts'.

Nannerl was twenty-five years old, Wolfgang nineteen. The *Deutsche Chronik*, edited by the poet and musician Christian Friedrich Daniel Schubart, maintained that 'If Mozart is not a plant forced in the hothouse, he is bound to grow into one of the greatest musical composers who ever lived'.

In Salzburg between 1773 and 1776 Wolfgang wrote nearly a hundred works; including sonatas for piano, masses and arias, various canons, variations for piano on contemporary themes, serenades intended as finales at festivities and divertimenti for diverse occasions. In fact, Wolfgang composed everything that music-loving citizens of the town ordered or begged of him.

His father wrote again to the publishers Breitkopf and Härtel in Leipzig:

I beg you to inform me whether you will wish to publish something. I must, however, ask you to let me know soon, and also to add on what conditions you would undertake such publication so that we will not need to waste time in correspondence about these trifles.

Again there was no answer. While Wolfgang was alive not a single work of his was published by Breitkopf and Härtel. But seven years after his death they began to bring out a collection of his works.

Wolfgang always kept in touch with his much-loved teacher Padre Martini in Bologna. He sent him many compositions, asking him to let him know 'frankly and without reserve' what he thought of them, and wrote him frequent letters about his work.

We live in this world in order to learn industriously and, by interchanging our ideas, to enlighten one another and thus endeavour to promote the sciences and the fine arts. Oh, how often have I longed to be near you, most Reverend Father, so that I might be able to talk to and have discussion with you. For I live in a country where music leads a struggling existence, though indeed apart from those who have left us, we still have excellent teachers and particularly composers of great wisdom, learning and taste. As for the theatre, we are in a bad way for lack of singers. We have no castrati, and we shall never have them, because they insist on being handsomely paid; and generosity is not one of our faults. Meanwhile I am amusing myself by writing chamber music and music for the church, in which branches of composition we have two other excellent masters of counterpoint, Signori Haydn and Adlgasser. My father is in the service of the Cathedral and this gives me an opportunity of writing as much church music as I like. He has already served this court for thirty-six years and as he knows that the present Archbishop cannot and will not have anything to do with people who are getting on in years, he no longer puts his whole heart into his work, but has taken up literature, which was always a favourite study of his.

O, carissimo Signor Padre Maestro, if we were together, I should have so many things to tell you! I send my devoted remembrances to all the members of the Accademia Filarmonica. I long to win your favour and I never cease to grieve that I am far away from that one person in the world whom I love, revere and esteem most of all'.

The Tanzmeisterhaus where the Mozart family lived from 1773—1787

The Tanzmeistersaal (music room)

The Mozart family. Oil painting by Johann Nepomuk della Croce, winter 1780—1781

Wolfgang. Detail from the family portrait by della Croce

Michael Haydn

Johann Lorenz Hagenauer

Joachim Ferdinand von Schiedenhofen

Nannerl.
Detail from the
family portrait
by della Croce

Luise Robinig von
Rottenfeld

The mansion of the
Robinigs near Salzburg

Sigmund Haffner von Imbachhausen

Franz Xaver Anton Späth

Silvester Barisani

Although Wolfgang was only a concert master at the Archbishop's Court, he had many duties to perform. Count Colloredo was very fond of holding festive receptions and for these Wolfgang had to compose special music. For one important occasion, the visit to Salzburg of the Archduke Maximilian, Maria Theresa's youngest son, he composed the festive opera *Il Re pastore* to a libretto by Metastasio. Maximilian always remained a faithful supporter of Wolfgang.

Other works composed at that time were: several symphonies, a piano concerto, also one for three pianos, the 'Lodron' concerto, a concerto for two violins, five violin concertos, which were first played by the amateur Kolb and the court musician Brunetti, a bassoon concerto, liturgies and church sonatas.

Schiedenhofen was constantly in touch with Wolfgang and his work:

'To the Cathedral at five o'clock in the afternoon, for the sermon and for the Litany by Mozart.'

'Afterwards to the Cathedral, where His Grace officiated. The Mass was a new one by young Mozart.'

'After dinner to the music composed by Mozart for the Countess Ernst Lodron.'

'After dinner I went to the bridal music which young Herr Haffner had made for his sister Liserl. It was by Mozart and was performed in the summer house at Loreto.'

'At night, until 12 o'clock, I went for a walk with Carl Agliardi and others, and there was also music at Mozart's'.

Wolfgang could not bear the narrow atmosphere of his home town for long. The demands made on him were too limited. And the means to carry out these demands too meagre. He had given concerts at the greatest courts in Europe, composed for great opera houses. He had to find another field of activity.

On 1 August 1777 he handed a petition to the Archbishop:

. . . Our circumstances are pressing: my father decided to send me off by myself. But to this too Your Serene Highness made some gracious objections. Most gracious Sovereign Prince and Lord! Parents take pains to enable their children to earn their own bread, and this they owe both to their own interest and to that of the State. The more of talent that children have received from God, the greater is the obligation to make use thereof, in order to ameliorate their own and their parents' circumstances, to assist their parents, and to take care of their own advancement and future. Such usury with our talents is taught us by the Gospel. I therefore owe it before God and in my conscience to my father, who indefatigably employs all his

101

time in my upbringing, to be grateful to him with all my strength, to lighten his burden, and to take care not only of myself, but of my sister also, with whom I should be bound to commiserate for spending so many hours at the clavier without being able to make profitable use of it. May Your Serene Highness graciously permit me, therefore, to beg most submissively to be released from service . . .

The answer was 'Granted'. Sarcastically, the Archbishop noted on the margin of the petition that father and son had permission to seek their fortune elsewhere, 'according to the Gospel'.

Leopold begged for indulgence. His dismissal was withdrawn, and he remained in the service of the court. He sent Wolfgang, accompanied by his mother, on a journey. Somewhere Wolfgang would find his fortune. Wolfgang, too, was convinced of it.

On 23 September 1777, at six in the morning, mother and son set out. The father sent a letter after them:

I did all I could not to make our parting too painful. Nannerl wept bitterly and I did all I could to console her. In the rush and flurry I forgot to give my son a father's blessing. I ran to the window and sent my blessing after you both.

The guard-room of the Prince Archbishop's Residence

Maria Anna, Countess Lodron

Nikolaus Sebastian, Count Lodron

The Archduke Maximilian Franz of Austria

Detail from the Salzburg Court Calendar, 1775

Mozart's petition to Count Colloredo, 1 August 1777

Whenever Leopold had undertaken a journey the material success had been certain. Maria Anna Mozart had neither her husband's talent for organisation nor his business sense. In their correspondence with Leopold it is obvious how helpless she and her son were on their journey. From Munich she wrote 'We have very many good friends who would like us to remain here'.
But Wolfgang added:

True enough! Any number of good friends, but unfortunately most of them can do little or nothing. I was with Count Seeau yesterday morning at half past ten and found him much more serious and not so frank as he was the first time. But it was only in appearance. Then today I called on Prince Zeill, who said to me in the most polite manner: 'I am afraid that we shall not accomplish very much here. When we were at table at Nymphenburg I had a few words in private with the Elector. He said: "It is too early yet. He ought to go off, travel to Italy and make a name for himself"'. So there we are! The Bishop of Chiemsee also had a word in private with the Electress, who, however, shrugged her shoulders and said that she would do her best, but was very doubtful.

A few days later he wrote:
I am very popular here. And how much more popular I should be if I could help forward the German national theatre!

Leopold replied sternly:

If that were immediately practicable, well and good, and you ought to accept a commission. But if you cannot obtain one at once then you simply must not lounge about, use up your money and waste your time.

Two days later he confessed:

What grieves me now and then is that I no longer hear you playing on the clavier or the violin; and whenever I enter our house a slight feeling of melancholy comes over me, for, as I approach the door, I think that I ought to be hearing you play.

Wolfgang and his mother left Munich on 11 October and arrived the same evening in Augsburg, where they put up at the White Lamb. Following his father's instructions Wolfgang visited Johann Andreas Stein, the famous organ and piano-forte maker, and wrote with great enthusiasm:
Before I had seen any of his make, Späth's claviers had always been my

favourites. But now I much prefer Stein's, for they damp ever so much better than the Regensburg instruments. When I strike hard, I can keep my fingers on the note or raise it, but the sound ceases the moment I have produced it. In whatever way I touch the keys, the tone is always even. It never jars, it is never stronger or weaker or entirely absent; in a word, it is always even. His instruments have this special advantage over others that they are made with escape action. Only one maker in a hundred bothers about this. But without an escapement it is impossible to avoid jangling and vibration after the note is struck. When you touch the keys, the hammers fall back again the moment after they have struck the strings, whether you hold down the keys or release them. He himself told me that when he has finished making one of these claviers, he sits down to it and tries all kinds of passages, runs and jumps. For he labours solely in the interest of music and not for his own profit.

They stayed in Augsburg till 26 October. He gave two concerts there but the most important event for him was his meeting with Maria Anna Thekla, the daughter of Leopold's brother Franz, the bookbinder. She wrote to her uncle in Salzburg:

> I cannot express our pleasure at the happy arrival of my aunt and such a darling cousin.

In high spirits Wolfgang related to his father how together they made fun of a priest, a certain Father Emilian: 'A conceited ass, he wanted to have fun with my cousin but she made fun of him.'
Leopold answered kindly:

> I am altogether delighted to hear that my niece is beautiful, sensible, charming, clever and gay, only it seems to me that she has too many friends among the priests.

Wolfgang replied somewhat ambiguously:
> My dear little cousin, who sends greetings to you both is nothing less than a morsel for priests.

On the day before he left he wrote in her album:
> Si vous aimés ce que j'aime
> Vous vous aimés donc vous même
> votre
> Très affectioné Neveu
> Wolfgang Amadé Mozart

After their parting, Wolfgang wrote several letters to his little cousin — the 'Bäsle' as he called her. Leopold's fear that the 'Bäsle' was on too familiar terms with the priests turned out to be justified. Indeed some years later she had an illegitimate daughter by one of them, the canon, Baron von Reibald. Like Wolfgang she was to die young, at the age of thirty-eight.

On 30 October 1777, Wolfgang and his mother arrived in Mannheim. The Court of the Elector Karl Theodor was at that time a great centre for music. The 'Mannheim School' bridged the gap from Baroque to classical music. Its founder, Johann Stamitz, had discovered a whole new range of orchestral expression: crescendo and diminuendo, tremolo, accent, glissando. Clarinet and woodwind players emerged, the minuet became part of the symphony.

Wolfgang made friends with Christian Cannabich who had been a pupil of Stamitz and was now the leader of the excellent court orchestra; and he met Georg Joseph Vogler and others who were working along those lines. He also got to know Ignaz Fränzl, the famous violinist, Anton Raaf, the tenor, who was later to sing Idomeneo in Munich, Anton Schweitzer, the composer and conductor, and Baron von Dalberg, the manager of the theatre who was, later on, the first man to stage Schiller's youthful plays.

Wolfgang was present at the rehearsals of the court orchestra. He went to the opera and to a French comedy. He gave a performance at Court in the presence of the Elector Karl Theodor, played the organ in the Court chapel and tried out the new one in the Protestant church.

> The orchestra is excellent and very strong. On either side there are ten or eleven violins, four violas, two oboes, two flutes and two clarinets, two horns, four violoncellos, four bassoons and four double basses, also trumpets and drums. They can produce fine music.

His father was anxious:

> If you get an opportunity of really showing what you can do, then you have hopes of remaining in Mannheim. I am sorry that we are now so far from one another. By the time I write to you about any matter, it is all over as far as you are concerned.

Whereupon Wolfgang had to admit:

> Yesterday I had to go with Cannabich to Count Savioli, the Intendant, to fetch my present. It was just as I had expected. No money, but a fine gold watch. At the moment ten carolins would have suited me better than

the watch. I now have five watches. I am therefore seriously thinking of having an additional watch pocket on each leg of my trousers, so that when I visit some great lord it will not occur to him to present me with another.

The following day it was Wolfgang who added a postscript to his mother's letter. He had something extremely important to divulge.

I, Johannes Chrysostomus Amadeus Wolfgangus Sigismundus Mozart, hereby plead guilty and confess that yesterday and the day before (not to mention on several other occasions) I did not get home until midnight; and that from ten o'clock until the said hour at Cannabich's house and in the presence and company of the said Cannabich, his wife and daughter, the Treasurer, Ramm and Lang I did frequently, without any difficulty, but quite easily, perpetrate — rhymes, the same being, moreover, sheer garbage. I should not have behaved so godlessly, however, if our ringleader, known under the name of Lisel (Elisabetha Cannabich), had not egged me on and incited me; at the same time I must admit that I thoroughly enjoyed it.

It was impossible for his father to be happy about such postscripts:

The object of your journey, the very necessary object was and is and must be, to obtain an appointment or to make money. So far I see little prospect of the one or the other; unless, of course, it has to be kept a secret from me.

That was written on 27 November. In his letter for the New Year of 1778, Wolfgang tried to make it up with his father, and begged him most humbly to think better of him.

In the letters from Mannheim, he had frequently mentioned Rosa Cannabich, to whom he was giving piano lessons. She was the second daughter of his friend Cannabich and was only thirteen years old. Wolfgang composed for her too. But then — on 17 January, after telling his father about a certain Herr Weber who was copying some music for him, he went on to ask:

I don't know whether I have already written about his daughter or not — She sings indeed most admirably and has a lovely, pure voice. The only thing she lacks is dramatic action; were it not for that, she might be the prima donna on any stage. She is only sixteen.

She was Aloysia Weber, and hardly three weeks passed before he confessed:

I have become so fond of this unfortunate family that my dearest wish is to make them happy; and perhaps I may be able to do so. My advice is that they should go to Italy. So now I should like you to write to our good friend Lugiati, and the sooner the better, and enquire what are the highest terms given to a prima donna in Verona — the more the better, one can always climb down — perhaps too it would be possible to obtain a contract for Ascension Day in Venice. As far as her singing is concerned, I would wager my life that she will bring me renown. Even in a short time she has greatly profited by my instruction, and how much greater will the improvement be by then! I am not anxious either about her acting. If our plan succeeds, we, M. Weber, his two daughters and I will have the honour of visiting my dear Papa and my dear sister for a fortnight on our way through Salzburg.

Leopold read of his son's ideas 'with horror'.

The whole night long I was unable to sleep and am so exhausted that I can only write quite slowly, word by word. This letter, in which I only recognise my son by that failing of his which makes him believe everyone at the first word spoken, open his kind heart to every plausible flatterer and let others sway him as they like — this letter, I say, depressed me exceedingly.

What impresario would not laugh, were one to recommend him a girl of sixteen or seventeen, who has never yet appeared on a stage! As for your proposal (I can hardly write when I think of it), your proposal to travel about with Herr Weber and, be it noted, his two daughters — it has nearly made lose my reason! My dearest son! How can you have allowed yourself to be bewitched even for an hour by such a horrible idea, which must have been suggested to you by someone or other! Your letter reads like a romance. For could you really make up your mind to go trailing about the world with strangers? Quite apart from your reputation — what of your old parents and your dear sister?

Off with you to Paris! and that soon! Find your place among great people. Aut Caesar aut nihil. The mere thought of seeing Paris ought to have preserved you from all these flighty ideas. From Paris the name and fame of a man of great talent resounds throughout the whole world.

The Bavarian Elector Maximilian Joseph III with Joseph Anton, Count Seeau, director of music and theatre

Ferdinand Christoph
Count Waldburg-Zeil,
Prince Bishop of Chiemsee

Johann Andreas Stein

Maria Anna Thekla Mozart,
the 'Bäsle'

This is how Mozart drew her

Christian Cannabich

Anton Schweitzer

The Paradeplatz, Mannheim

The Elector Karl Theodor, patron of the Mannheim School

Ignaz Fränzl

Georg Joseph Vogler

Anton Raaff

Wolfgang Heribert
von Dalberg

114

Letter of Maria Anna to her husband Leopold Mozart with Wolfgang's postscript: 'I, Johannes Chrisostomus Amadeus Wolfgangus Sigismundus Mozart . . .'

Aloysia Weber

Wolfgang and his mother took exactly six months to reach Paris. In order to finance their journey Leopold had run into debt. Their earnings had been negligible. In Mannheim Wolfgang had composed various arias — for the tenor Raaf and for Aloysia, for the wife and daughter of the flautist Wendling. He had composed piano sonatas, an oboe concerto, two flute concertos, some flute quartets and a Mass, of which only the Kyrie is preserved. The purpose of the journey, however, which was to find employment, had remained unfulfilled.

On 23 March 1778 they arrived in Paris. It was fifteen years since he had been there as a child, and now no one was waiting to spoil him or even to make him welcome. Still Paris remained his great hope. He wrote to Salzburg: 'I trust that with the help of God all will be well'.

Mother and son moved into humble lodgings. As an opening Wolfgang arranged Holzbauer's 'Miserere' for a performance in Holy Week at the 'Concert Spirituel', the most important musical institution in Paris. The director, Le Gros, also asked him to write a concert symphony but then refused to perform it.

The exchange of letters between Wolfgang and his father has an unhappy tone; Leopold harangued his son, Wolfgang tried to pacify him and explain:

Leopold: I now urge you very strongly to win, or rather to preserve by a complete childlike trust, the favour, affection and friendship of Baron Grimm, to consult him in all matters, not to act on your own judgment or preconceived ideas, and constantly to bear in mind your interest and in this way our common interest. The mode of living in Paris is very different from that in Germany.

Wolfgang: I told Grimm all about it. You say I ought to pay a good many calls in order to make new acquaintances and revive the old ones. That, however, is quite out of the question. The distances are too great for walking — or the roads too muddy — for really the mud in Paris is beyond all description. To take a carriage means that you have the honour of spending four to five livres a day, and all for nothing. People pay plenty of compliments, it is true, but there it ends. If only this were a place where people had ears to hear, hearts to feel and some measure of understanding for music.

Leopold: I know by experience that in Paris you have to pay a hundred calls for nothing and indeed I told you this long ago. Further, I am well aware that the French people pay in compliments. Moreover, it is an undeniable fact that everywhere you will have enemies, inasmuch as all men of great talent have them.

Wolfgang: Noverre is going to arrange a new ballet for which I am going to compose the music. Rodolphe (who plays the French horn) is in Royal service here and is a very good friend of mine. He has offered me the post of organist at Versailles, if I will accept it. The salary is 2000 livres a year, but I should have to spend six months at Versailles and the other six in Paris, or wherever I like. I do not think that I shall accept it. After all, 2000 livres is not such a big sum. It would be so in German money, I admit, but here it is not. It is frightful how quickly a thaler disappears here.

Leopold: So Rodolphe has offered you the post of organist at Versailles? Does the appointment rest with him? If so, he will surely help you to get it! You must not throw that away so lightly. You must bear in mind that you would be earning eighty-three louis d'or in six months — and that you would have another six months in which to make money in other ways. Further, it is probably a life appointment, I mean, that you hold it whether you are well or ill — and, moreover, that you can always resign it. You should remember too that you would be at Court and therefore nearer your goal, and that you might later obtain one of the two posts of Kapellmeister. Read what I say to Baron Grimm and get his opinion.

Wolfgang: I am tolerably well, thank God, but I often wonder whether life is worth living — I am neither hot nor cold — and don't find much pleasure in anything.

Leopold: There is no reason whatever why you should be unhappy. God has bestowed great talents upon you. You were desperately impatient to leave Salzburg. At last you are in a city where, even though everything is exceptionally dear, a lot of money can be made. But pains and hard work are necessary! In short, if events do not shape themselves as you want and expect them to, remember that in this world it has always been and always will be thus, and that this is something to which everyone, from beggar to king, must submit.

Waiting at the doors of the rich and influential — time dragged on. Kind words were all they gave him. The Duc de Guines commissioned a concerto for flute and harp, and engaged him as a teacher for his daughter. Wolfgang complained to his father:

For the last four weeks the Duke has had my concerto, for which he has not yet paid me.

To Aloysia in Mannheim he wrote:

Addio for the present, dearest friend, I am anxious to get a letter from you. Please do not keep me waiting and do not make me suffer too long.

In June Wolfgang's mother fell ill. The doctor came to bleed her. On the same evening, the 11th, Noverre's ballet, *Les petits riens*, had its first performance. The Parisian press reported the occasion. Noverre's choreography was praised, Mozart's music received no mention.

Baron Grimm wrote to Leopold Mozart in Salzburg: that the reason for his son's failure might lie in the ridiculous quarrel between the Gluckists and the Piccinni-ists who kept the whole of Paris in suspense. No one could spare the time for any other musician.

Wolfgang's mother was unable to leave the house now. She was unable to hear the Symphony in D major, the 'Paris' Symphony, which was performed at the Concert Spirituel in the Tuileries. Her illness had been sudden. On 14 and again on 29 May she had written to Salzburg, that — thank God — she was well. On 12 June she had written 'Thank God, Wolfgang and I are well. I was bled yesterday, so I shan't be able to write much today'. But on 3 July Wolfgang began his letter to his father with the news 'My dear mother is ill'. On the same day he wrote to his friend, the Abbé Bullinger, in Salzburg:

Most beloved Friend! For you alone.

Mourn with me, my friend! This has been the saddest day of my life — I am writing this at two o'clock in the morning. I have to tell you that my mother, my dear mother, is no more! God has called her to Himself. It was His will to take her, that I saw clearly — so I resigned myself to His will. He gave her to me, so He was able to take her away from me. Only think of all my anxiety, the fears and sorrows I have had to endure for the last fortnight. She was quite unconscious at the time of her death — her life flickered out like a candle. Three days before her death she made her confession, partook of the Sacrament and received Extreme Unction. During the last three days, however, she was constantly delirious, and today at twenty-one minutes past five o'clock the death agony began and she lost all sensation and consciousness. I pressed her hand and spoke to her — but she did not see me, she did not hear me, and all feeling was gone. She lay thus until she expired five hours later at twenty-one minutes past ten. No one was present but myself, Herr Heina (a kind friend whom my father knows) and the nurse. It is quite impossible for me to describe today the whole course of her illness, but I am firmly convinced that she was bound to die and that God had so ordained it. All I ask of you at present is to act the part of a true friend, by preparing my poor father very gently for this sad news. I have written to him by this post, but only to say that she is seriously ill; and now I shall wait for his answer and be guided by it. May God give him strength and courage! O my friend! Not only am I now comforted, but I have been comforted for some time. By the mercy of God I have borne it all with fortitude and composure. When her illness became dangerous, I prayed to God for two things only — a happy death for her and strength and courage for myself; and God in His goodness heard my prayer and gave me those two blessings in the richest measure. I beg you, therefore, most beloved friend, watch over my father for me and try to give him courage so that, when he hears the worst, he may not take it too hardly. I commend my sister to you also with all my heart. Go to them both at once, I implore you — but do not tell them yet that she is dead — just prepare them for it. Do what you think best — use every means to comfort them — but so act that my mind may be relieved — and that I may not have to dread another blow. Watch over my dear father and my dear sister for me. Send me a reply at once, I entreat you. Adieu. I remain your most obedient and grateful servant

Wolfgang Amadé Mozart.

Wolfgang hesitated for six days, then he wrote and told his father.

On that very same day, the 3rd, at twenty-one minutes past ten at night my mother fell asleep peacefully in the Lord; indeed, when I wrote to you, she was already enjoying the blessings of Heaven — for all was then over. I wrote to you during that night and I hope that you and my dear sister will forgive me for this slight but very necessary deception; for as I judged from my own grief and sorrow what yours would be, I could not indeed bring myself suddenly to shock you with this dreadful news! Remember that Almighty God willed it thus — and how can we rebel against Him? In those distressing moments, there were three things that consoled me — entire and steadfast submission to the will of God, and the sight of her very easy and beautiful death. Indeed I wished at that moment to depart with her. From this wish and longing proceeded finally my third source of consolation — the thought that she is not lost to us for ever.

From the church register of Saint-Eustache:

4 July 1778 — On the said day, Marie-Anne Pertl, aged 57 years, wife of Leopold Mozart, maître de chapelle at Salzburg, was interred in the cemetery in the presence of Wolfgang Amadée Mozart, her son, and of Francois Heina, trumpeter.

Wolfgang could not establish himself in Paris and to make matters worse he quarrelled with Baron Grimm. Both complained in their letters to Salzburg:

Wolfgang: He is not the same as he was.
Grimm: Let him start by giving piano-lessons, — but he won't.
Wolfgang: He may be able to help children but not grown-up people.
Grimm: He must show some enterprise . . .
Wolfgang: Stupidly, boorishly, he talked to me.
Grimm: Much too naive . . .
Wolfgang: Base.
Grimm: much too inactive.
Wolfgang: he is not my true friend.

Mozart broke with Baron Grimm, and on 26 September he left Paris. The return to Salzburg meant humiliation. But there was no other way.

In Mannheim he stayed with the Cannabich family. Then he travelled on to Munich. He took his time. He had no desire to get back to Salzburg, it was not his goal; at the most it was a refuge for the defeated. In Munich he met the Weber family again. They had moved here from Mannheim. Aloysia had an engagement at the Opera and was the mistress of the Elector. She wanted nothing more to do with Mozart. She ridiculed the mourning buttons on his coat, considered him piteous. Deeply hurt, Wolfgang spent days locked in the house of his friend, Johann Baptist Becke, the flautist. Becke was worried about him and wrote to Leopold 'He is assailed by some fear lest your reception of him may not be as tender as he wishes . . . '

The return journey from Paris to Salzburg took three and a half months, and for the first time he travelled alone. He was then twenty-two years old. Since he was six he had spent eleven years travelling around in Europe and only five at home in Salzburg. He spoke four languages. He had studied with many great musicians of this time. He had been active in England and France, in Italy, Belgium, Holland, Switzerland, in Germany and Vienna. He was no longer the spoilt prodigy, but the young, self-willed genius, whom no court, no ruler wanted to employ. 'He ought to go and make a name for himself' said the Bavarian Elector. 'If he were less gifted, he would make his fortune' said Baron Grimm. 'Let him write short, light, popular pieces' said his father. Mozart's flight from Salzburg ended in Salzburg.

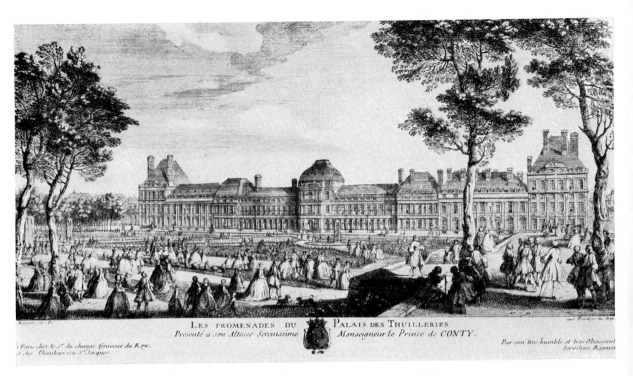

The Tuileries, where the performances of the Concert Spirituel took place

Joseph le Gros

Adrien-Louis de Bounières, Duc de Guines

(*Above*) Christoph Willibald Gluck (*Below*) Nicola Piccinni

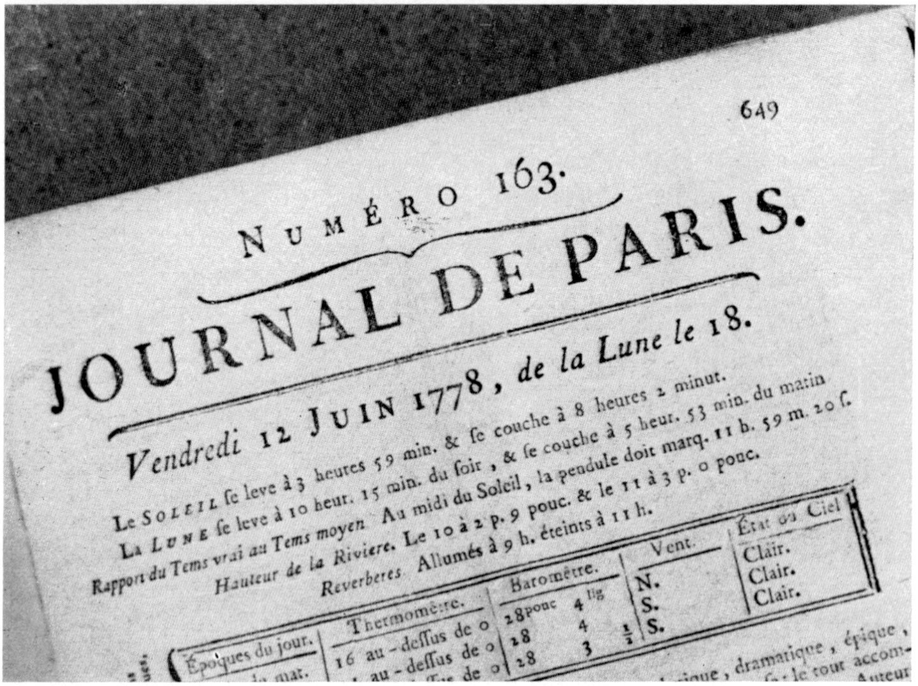

649

NUMÉRO 163.

JOURNAL DE PARIS.

Vendredi 12 JUIN 1778, de la Lune le 18.

Le SOLEIL se leve à 3 heures 59 min. & se couche à 8 heures 2 minut.
La LUNE se leve à 10 heur. 15 min. du soir, & se couche à 5 heur. 53 min. du matin
Rapport du Tems vrai au Tems moyen. Au midi du Soleil, la pendule doit marq. 11 h. 59 m. 20 s.
Hauteur de la Riviere. Le 10 à 2 p. 9 pouc. & le 11 à 3 p. 0 pouc.
Reverberes. Allumés à 9 h. éteints à 11 h.

Epoques du jour.	Thermométre.	Barométre.		Vent.	État du Ciel
le mat.	16 au-dessus de o	28 pouc	4 lig	N.	Clair.
	au-dessus de o	18	4	S. S.	Clair.
	au-dessus de o	18	3	S.	Clair.

The leading Paris newspaper

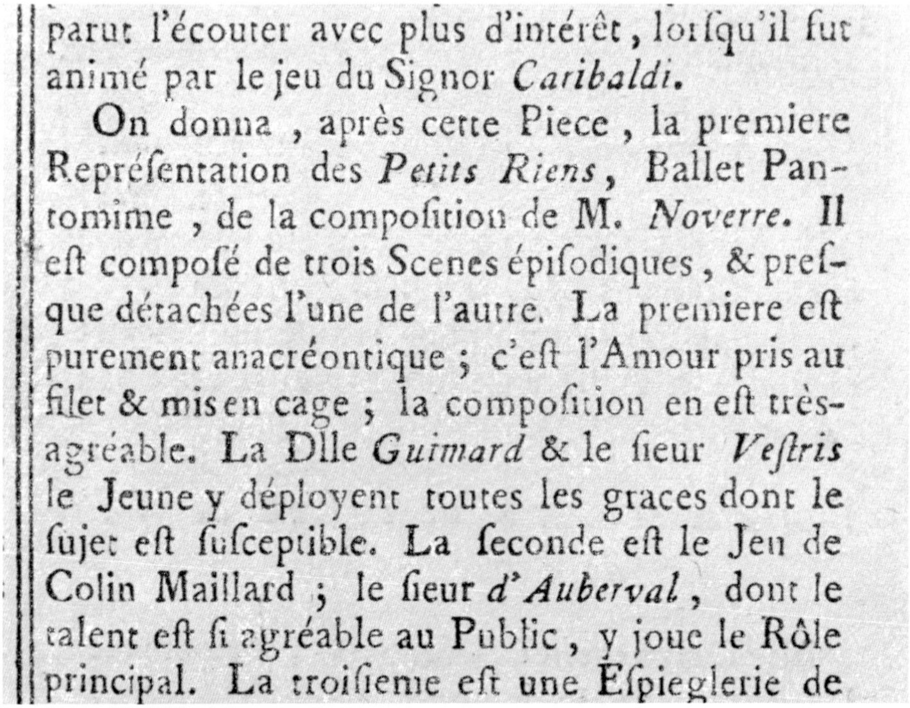

parut l'écouter avec plus d'intérêt, lorsqu'il fut animé par le jeu du Signor *Caribaldi*.

On donna, après cette Piece, la premiere Représentation des *Petits Riens*, Ballet Pantomime, de la composition de M. *Noverre*. Il est composé de trois Scenes épisodiques, & presque détachées l'une de l'autre. La premiere est purement anacréontique ; c'est l'Amour pris au filet & mis en cage ; la composition en est très-agréable. La Dlle *Guimard* & le sieur *Vestris* le Jeune y déployent toutes les graces dont le sujet est susceptible. La seconde est le Jeu de Colin Maillard ; le sieur *d'Auberval*, dont le talent est si agréable au Public, y joue le Rôle principal. La troisieme est une Espieglerie de

Extract from the review of the ballet, 'Les petits riens'. Mozart's name is not mentioned

126

Wolfgang's letter to his father about his mother's death

The churchyard of L'Eglise des Innocents, Paris

Mozart's mother, from the family portrait by della Croce

Even before Wolfgang reached Salzburg his father had drawn up a petition on his behalf to the Archbishop asking for him to be reinstated in court service. Wolfgang had only to sign it. Two days after his return, on 17 January 1779, he handed it in:

Your Serene Highness! Most Reverend Prince of the Holy Roman Empire! Most Gracious Sovereign Prince and Lord!

Your Serene Highness was most graciously pleased after the decease of Cajetan Adlgasser most graciously to take me into your service: I therefore most submissively beg that I may be graciously assigned the post of Court Organist in your Exalted Service; to which end, as for all other high favours and graces, I subscribe myself in the most profound submission,

Your Serene Highness, my most gracious Sovereign Prince and Lord's most submissive and most obedient   Wolfgang Amadé Mozart.

On 26 February he received the official reply:

Whereas We by these presents have graciously admitted and accepted the suppliant as Our Court Organist, that he shall, like Adlgasser, carry out his appointed duties with diligent assiduity and irreproachably, in the Cathedral as well as at Court and in the Chapel, and shall as far as possible serve the Court and the Church with new compositions made by him; We decree him therefore, like his predecessor, an annual salary of four hundred and fifty florins, and command Our Court Pay Office to discharge this by monthly instalments, and to render account for each outlay in the appropriate place.   Hieronymus m. p.

His salary now, at the age of twenty-four, was the same as that of an Episcopal Court Councillor. During the time that followed, he wrote the concerto for two pianos in E flat, the symphony concertante for violin and viola, and symphonies in G, B and C major in three movements. He composed the Coronation Mass and the Missa Solemnis in C, two Vespers, other smaller liturgical works and a series of church sonatas for organ and orchestra, a serenade and a divertimento, both in D major.

Once more the social life of Salzburg with its modest entertainments enveloped him. At the theatre he had the opportunity of seeing Böhn's company in several plays including *Minna von Barnhelm* and *Romeo and Juliet*. Another visiting company was under the direction of the impressario Emanuel Schikaneder with whom the Mozart family became friendly. Schikaneder, born in Regensburg in 1751, started out as a wandering musician and later became an actor, singer and producer. In 1778 he had formed his own company and had arrived in Salzburg via Stuttgart, Nuremberg and Linz. Wolfgang was to collaborate with him later on *Die Zauberflöte*.

Wolfgang could not be happy in Salzburg which was, as he had said 'no place for his talent'. The monotony of the everyday life of the town is apparent in the diary which Nannerl kept:

> The Month of April.
> The 1st: In the Cathedral at Mass, afterwards breakfasted at Salerl's I and my brother. Afterwards with my brother at Court to see 'The Last Supper', in the afternoon with Catherl in the College, the Hospital, St. Peter, in the Cathedral for silent Mass, afterwards home, we played.
> The 2nd: At Catherl's with my brother for breakfast at eight o'clock, together with her in the Cathedral, afterwards did the 'Holy Steps', afterwards St. Johannes, St. Andre, St. Sebastian, afterwards at lunch. After lunch at the Collegio, at Catherl's, in the Cathedral. At six o'clock Catherl came to us, funeral music at the Holy Trinity.
> The 9th: At seven o'clock Mass, afterwards at Oberbreitter's, and Frau von Mayer. In the afternoon at Fraulein's. In the evening Herr Bauer at our house.
> The 10th: At the Requiem at St. Sebastian. Afterwards at Mayer's. Afternoon Fraulein.
> The 11th: At seven o'clock Mass, Herr Paris eat with us. Bullinger best cards. Papa won. Afterwards at the play.
> The 14th: At the play.
> The 15th: In the evening the young Herr von Weinrotter at our house.

Sometimes Wolfgang took over:

> The twentieth — at the seven o'clock Mass. Afterwards at Fräulein and Frau von Mayer, after the meal at Catherl's, old Hagenauer, then home. At six o'clock with Papa and Pimperl for a constitutional, Catherl with Bauer running after us — chatted with Stierle and his wife — the sun slunk into a sack — at ten o'clock it rained, with pleasant stink — smell — the clouds got lost, the moon let herself be seen, giving hope of nice weather for the morrow's day, for which we are so anxious.

In September 1779 Wolfgang wrote in the diary:

> Rained the whole day — at nine o'clock in the Cathedral, prayed an

Mozart's petition to the Prince Archbishop Count Colloredo, 17 January, 1779

The staircase to the organ loft, Salzburg Cathedral

hour — played Tarot — At two o'clock at Lodron's — played Tarot — At half past seven in Church, and called at Barisani to congratulate. The whole day alternately heavy showers, — played Tarot — the evening charming.

At last an invitation from Munich broke the monotony. The Elector, Karl Theodor, who had succeeded the Bavarian Elector Maximilian Joseph III, knew Mozart from his days in Mannheim and now commissioned him to write a festive opera for the Carnival, *Idomeneo*.

Wolfgang started work immediately. The Archbishop was unwilling to grant him leave but for political reasons he could not refuse. He needed the goodwill of the Bavarian Elector. Wolfgang arrived in Munich on 6 November, completed the opera and conducted the first rehearsals. Many of the Court musicians from Mannheim including Cannabich and Raaf had moved to Munich with the Elector, and the Munich orchestra was now one of the best to be heard. Mozart appreciated this. His broad orchestral passages were written to suit the players.

The opera opened on 29 January. Leopold and Nannerl, and their friends Frau Robinig and Dr. Barisani and his wife came over from Salzburg for the occasion. But *Idomeneo* did not achieve the same kind of success as the Italian operas. There were only two repeat performances.

In a Munich newspaper of 1 February 1781 we find eleven lines about the opera. Seven are devoted to the praise of Lorenzo Quaglio's décor. The name of Mozart is not mentioned. It says: 'The text, music and translation are contributions from Salzburg.' The Elector's words about the composition were: 'One wouldn't believe such greatness to be tucked in such a little head'.

During his stay in Munich Wolfgang wrote the Serenade for thirteen wind instruments, the Kyrie in D minor, the oboe quartet and several songs and arias. His leave had come to an end; he should have been back in Salzburg. But in the meantime the Archbishop had gone to Vienna and so Wolfgang, Leopold and Nannerl stayed on in Munich.

Once again Leopold wrote to Breitkopf und Härtel in Leipzig:

I have the honour of writing to you from Munich, where I am on account of the opera which my son wrote for the Elector's theatre. I have been wishing for a long time that you would print some of my son's compositions. You might try and start with a couple of symphonies or piano sonatas, or even quartets, trios and so forth. You need only give us a few copies. I should very much like you to see my son's style of composition. But far be it from me to persuade you to anything.

The Prince Archbishop now ordered Wolfgang to come to Vienna. He had taken some of his musicians to the capital where he planned to hold receptions.

133

He needed his most talented musician. And so, on 16 March 1781, Wolfgang arrived in Vienna. On the following day he wrote to his father describing his journey and arrival:

I travelled in the mailcoach as far as Unterhaag — but by that time I was so sore in my behind and its surrounding parts that I could endure it no longer. So I was intending to proceed by the ordinaire, but Herr Escherich, a government official, had had enough of the mail coach too and gave me his company as far as Kemmelbach. From there I proceeded by extra-post.

I have a charming room in the very same house where the Archbishop is staying. We lunch about twelve o'clock, unfortunately somewhat too early for me. Our party consists of the two valets, that is, the body and soul attendants of His Worship, the contrôleur, Herr Zetti, the confectioner, the two cooks, Ceccarelli, Brunetti and — my insignificant self. By the way, the two valets sit at the top of the table, but at least I have the honour of being placed above the cooks.

On the 24th Wolfgang complained:

How gladly would I give a public concert as is the custom here. But I know for certain that I would never get permission to do so — for just listen to this! You know that there is a society in Vienna which gives concerts for the benefit of the widows of musicians, at which every professional musician plays gratis. The orchestra is a hundred and eighty strong, because they win the favour both of the Emperor and of the public. I agreed at once, adding, however, that I must first obtain the consent of my Prince. *He would not permit me to take part.* All the nobility in Vienna have made a grievance of it.

The nobility interceded and the Archbishop finally gave his consent for Wolfgang to appear in the concert. But the relationship between the Archbishop and his organist deteriorated. On 4 April Wolfgang wrote to his father:

I told you in a recent letter that the Archbishop is a great hindrance to me here, for he has done me out of at least a hundred ducats, which I certainly would have made by giving a concert in the theatre. Why, the ladies themselves offered of their own accord to distribute the tickets.

A week later he wrote:

When I think that I must leave Vienna without bringing home at least a thousand florins, my heart is sore indeed. So, for the sake of a malevolent

Prince who plagues me every day and only pays me a lousy salary of four hundred florins, I am to kick away a thousand? When we had a grand concert in this house, the Archbishop sent each of us four ducats. At the last concert for which I composed a new rondo for Brunetti, a new sonata for myself, and also a new rondo for Ceccarelli, I received nothing. But what made me almost desperate was that the very same evening we had this foul concert I was invited to Countess Thun's, but of course could not go; and who should be there but the Emperor!

In this atmosphere of tension the Archbishop sent his musicians back to Salzburg. He also ordered Wolfgang to leave Vienna. Wolfgang declared that he could not travel since he wished to collect some outstanding fees. The Archbishop let him know that he had an urgent parcel for Salzburg to entrust to him. A most important matter. Mozart regretted that unfortunately he could not undertake this commission. The Archbishop summoned him to an interview which Wolfgang described to his father in great detail:

> When I entered the room, his first words were: 'Well, young fellow, when are you going off?' I: 'I intended to go to-night, but all the seats were already engaged.' Then he rushed full steam ahead, without pausing for breath — I was the most dissolute fellow he knew — no one served him so badly as I did — he called me a scoundrel, a rascal, a vagabond! At last my blood began to boil, I could no longer contain myself and I said, 'So Your Grace is not satisfied with me?' 'What, you dare to threaten me — you scoundrel? There is the door! Look out, for I will have nothing more to do with such a miserable wretch.' At last I said: 'Nor I with you!' 'Well, be off!' When leaving the room, I said: 'This is final. You shall have it to-morrow in writing.'

> Tell me now, most beloved father, did I not say the word too late rather than too soon? My honour is more precious to me than anything else and I know that it is so to you also. Please inform me soon of your approval, for that is the only thing which is still wanting to my present happiness.

Wolfgang handed his resignation to his immediate superior, the Chief Steward Count Arco. There was a dispute, a scene — Count Arco dismissed the court organist with a kick.

The letters which Leopold wrote to his son during these weeks are lost. Only Wolfgang's letters to Salzburg remain. On 12 May he wrote to justify himself:

> I did not know that I was a valet — and that was the last straw. I ought to have idled away a couple of hours every morning in the antechamber. True, I was often told that I ought to present myself, but I could never

remember that this was part of my duty, and I only turned up punctually whenever the Archbishop sent for me.

On the same day he wrote a second letter to his father:

I shall say nothing whatever about all the injustice with which the Archbishop has treated me from the very beginning of his reign until now, of the incessant abuse, of all the impertinances and sottises which he has uttered to my face, of my undeniable right to leave him — for that cannot be disputed. I shall only speak of what would have induced me to leave him even without any cause of offence. I have here the finest and most useful acquaintances in the world. I am liked and respected by the greatest families. All possible honour is shown me and I am paid into the bargain. So why should I pine away in Salzburg for the sake of four hundred florins?

On 16 May:

I implore you, by all you hold dear in this world, to strengthen me in this resolution instead of trying to dissuade me from it. I have every confidence that I shall be more useful to you in Vienna than if I were to return to Salzburg.

On 19 May:

You say that I have never shown you any affection and therefore ought now to show it for the first time. Can you really say this? You add that I will never sacrifice any pleasures for your sake. But what pleasures have I here? The pleasure of taking trouble and pains to fill my purse? You seem to think I am revelling in pleasures and amusements. Oh how you deceive yourself indeed!

On 26 May:

It seems as if good fortune is about to welcome me here, and now I feel that I *must* stay. Indeed, I felt that when I left Munich. Without knowing why, I looked forward most eagerly to Vienna. You must be patient for a little while longer and then I shall be able to prove to you how useful Vienna is going to be to us all.

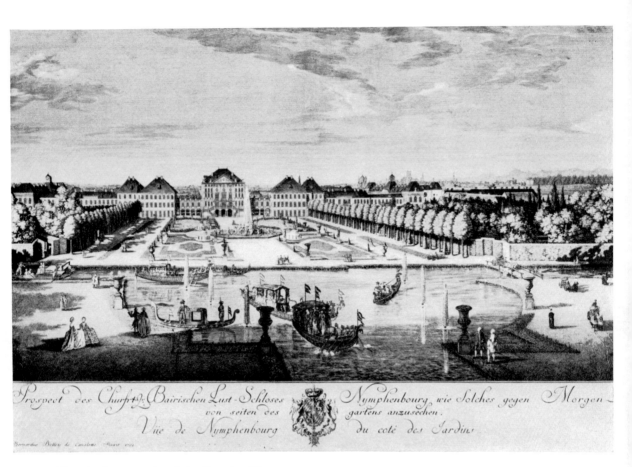

Prospect des Churfrtl. Bairischen Lust-Schloses zu Nymphenbourg, wie Solches gegen Morgen von seiten des gartens anzusehen.

Vüe de Nymphenbourg du coté des Jardins

Nymphenburg, castle of the Bavarian Elector

The overture to *Idomeneo* in Mozart's hand

Review of the first performance of *Idomeneo* in Munich

138

Schönbrunn Castle, Vienna

The theatre by the Kärntnertor, Vienna

The Emperor Joseph II

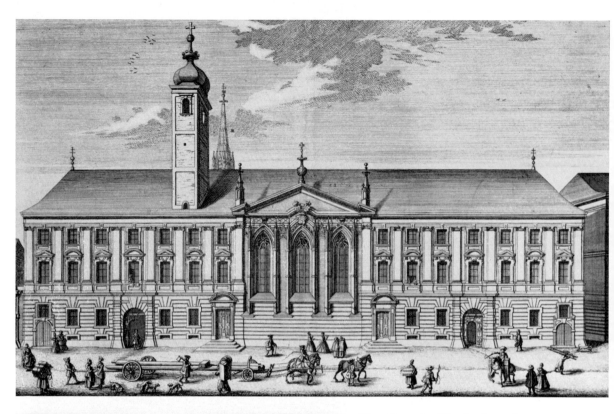

The 'Deutsche Haus' where the Prince Archbishop of Salzburg stayed on his visit to Vienna

Mozart's employer, Count Colloredo

The last page of Mozart's letter to his father about his break with Count Colloredo, dated 8 May 1780

This was a busy time for Wolfgang. He wrote to his sister:

I described my manner of life the other day to my father and I will repeat it to you. My hair is always done by six o'clock in the morning and by seven I am fully dressed. I then compose until nine. From nine to one I give lessons. Then I lunch, unless I am invited to some house where they lunch at two or even three o'clock, as, for example, today and tomorrow at Countess Zichy's and Countess Thun's. I can never work before five or six o'clock in the evening, and even then I am often prevented by a concert. If I am not prevented, I compose until nine.

He wrote violin sonatas, variations for violin and piano, piano sonatas, a sonata for two pianos, a concert-rondo for piano and orchestra, and serenades.

On 30 July Gottlieb Stephanie, a producer and dramatist at the Burgtheater, gave him a libretto: he was to compose an opera, *Die Entführung aus dem Serail*.

Wolfgang informed his father:

The time is short, it is true, for it is to be performed in the middle of September; but the circumstances connected with the date of performance and, in general, all my other prospects stimulate me to such a degree that I rush to my desk with the greatest eagerness and remain seated there with the greatest delight. The Grand Duke of Russia is coming here, and that is why Stephanie entreated me, if possible, to compose the opera in this short space of time.

While he was at work he wrote the now famous sentence to his father: 'In an opera the poetry must perforce be the obedient daughter of the music.'

He collaborated closely with the librettist:

As the original text began with a monologue, I asked Herr Stephanie to make a little arietta out of it — and then to put in a duet instead of making the two chatter together after Osmin's short song. As we have given the part of Osmin to Herr Fischer, who certainly has an excellent bass voice, we must take advantage of it, particularly as he has the whole Viennese public on his side. But in the original libretto Osmin has only this short song and nothing else to sing, except in the trio and the finale; so he has been given an aria in Act I, and he is to have another in Act II.

On 16 July 1782, the opera had its first performance and was a tremendous success. It was repeated on the 19th.

The takings for the two evenings were twelve hundred florins. *The Abduction from the Seraglio* has been hailed by the public from its first night until today. Its opening in Vienna was soon followed by performances in other cities: Warsawa, Riga, Breslau, Prague, Pressburg, Dresden, Weimar, Frankfurt, Munich, Aachen, Mannheim, Bonn, Mainz. But only those wanted to, paid Mozart. He was famous once more, and yet you have to search for his name on the playbills; it was in such very small print.

At the same time, Bretzner, on whose play Stephanie had based his libretto, openly protested against the misuse of his work:

> A certain individual, Mozart by name, in Vienna has had the audacity to misuse my drama 'Belmonte und Constanze' for an opera text. I herewith protest most solemnly against this infringement of my rights, and reserve the right to take the matter further.

The composer was held in no great esteem in those days. His work could be stolen by anyone. There was no copyright protection and the works of the masters were eagerly awaited by plagiarists. But Mozart forestalled them with his *Seraglio*. He himself arranged melodies from his opera for the popular music of woodwind and brass in order not to lose this income to others.

After *The Abduction from the Seraglio* Mozart became the most sought-after musician in Vienna. People rushed to be taught by him. The houses of the nobility and of the rich citizens opened their doors to him. Society ladies, mothers — and daughters — became his pupils. There was also a young man from Bonn on the Rhine who wanted to learn with him. His name was Ludwig van Beethoven. But Wolfgang's heart was not in teaching nor did the ladies of high society interest him so much as Constanze Weber, the sister of Aloysia, his old love.

There is no doubt that Constanze's mother had tried to lure the famous young man into her net. Even before his break with the Archbishop, Mozart had left the house of the Teutonic Order, where he was staying, the 'Deutsches Haus', and became a lodger at Frau Cäcilia Weber's, on the second floor of her house, 'Zum Auge Gottes'. His father had read of this with great suspicion and Wolfgang had promised to look for another place.

25 July 1781: I should very much like to know what pleasure certain people can find in spreading entirely groundless reports. Because I am living with them, therefore I am going to marry the daughter. If ever there was a time when I thought less of getting married, it is most certainly now!

1 August: The room into which I am moving is being got ready.

22 August: I cannot let you know the address of my new lodging, as I have not yet got one. But I am bargaining about the prices of two.

On 15 December he confessed:

But who is the object of my love? Do not be horrified again, I entreat you. Surely not one of the Webers? Yes, one of the Webers — but not Josepha, nor Sophie, but Constanze, the middle one. In no other family have I ever come across such differences of character. The eldest is a lazy, gross per-fidious woman, and as cunning as a fox. The youngest — is still too young to be anything in particular — she is just a good-natured, but featherheaded creature! May God protect her from seduction! But the middle one, my good, dear Constanze, is the martyr of the family and, probably for that very reason, is the kindest-hearted, the cleverest and, in short, the best of them all. She makes herself responsible for the whole household and yet in their opinion she does nothing right. Oh, my most beloved father, I could fill whole sheets with descriptions of all the scenes that I have witnessed in that house. If you want to read them, I shall do so in my next letter. But before I cease to plague you with my chatter, I must make you better acquainted with the character of my dear Constanze. She is not ugly, but at the same time far from beautiful. Her whole beauty consists in two little black eyes and a pretty figure. She has no wit, but she has enough common sense to enable her to fulfil her duties as a wife and mother. It is a down-right lie that she is inclined to be extravagant. On the contrary, she is accustomed to be shabbily dressed, for the little that her mother has been able to do for her children, she has done for the two others, but never for Constanze. True, she would like to be neatly and cleanly dressed, but not smartly, and most things that a woman needs she is able to make for herself; and she dresses her own hair every day. Moreover she understands house-keeping and has the kindest heart in the world. I love her and she loves me with all her heart. Tell me whether I could wish myself a better wife?

One thing more I must tell you, which is that when I resigned the Arch-bishop's service, our love had not yet begun. It was born of her tender care and attentions when I was living in their house.

On 4 August 1782, Wolfgang Amadeus Mozart married Constanze Weber. The wedding took place in the Stephansdom. He was twenty-six, she was twenty. He had not waited for his father's permission. He wrote and told him:

When we had been joined together, both my wife and I began to weep. All present, even the priest, were deeply touched and all wept to see how much our hearts were moved.

The first child of the marriage died, at eight weeks old. The second, a son, called Karl, remained alive. The third, also a boy, lived for four weeks. The fourth, a girl, died when she was six months old. The fifth only lived one hour. The sixth, another boy, Franz, born in the year of his father's death remained alive. Later his mother was to call him Wolfgang Amadeus II.

The newly-married Mozart had his hands full. He conducted concerts in the Burgtheater. He shone as a pianist at the Kärntnertor Theatre. He took part in the social life of Vienna. He played before the Emperor, before Count Esterházy, the Court Councillor, a great patron of music in his time, and in the house of Joseph Haydn. He was a guest of the Russian Ambassador, of Gluck, of many court officials and rich families. At a masked ball in the Assembly room of the palace he dressed up as an Indian philosopher and handed to the Viennese dignitaries verses like this one: 'It is not seemly for everybody to be modest; only great men are able to be so.' The publishers and music dealers wanted to make money and fought for his works. Everyone asked for Mozart.

On 23 March in the presence of the Emperor at the Imperial Theatre, he gave the first of a series of 'Grand Musical Concerts'. The *Magazin der Musik* reported the occasion:

" To-night the famous Herr Chevalier Mozart held a musical concert in the National Theatre, at which pieces of his already highly admired composition were performed. The concert was honoured with an exceptionally large concourse, and the two new concertos and other fantasies which Herr Mozart played on the fortepiano were received with the loudest applause. Our Monarch, who, against his habit, attended the whole of the concert, as well as the entire audience, accorded him such unanimous applause as has never been heard of here. The receipts of the concert are estimated to amount to 1,600 florins in all. "

And yet Wolfgang had worries. He did not know how to handle money. He spent it as soon as he earned it; nor was Constanze a careful housewife. On 15 February 1783, he was forced to write to the Baroness von Waldstätten, who had been his patron from his very first days in Vienna:

Most highly esteemed Baroness!
Here I am in a fine dilemma! Herr von Tranner and I discussed the matter the other day and agreed to ask for an extension of a fortnight. As every merchant does this, unless he is the most disobliging man in the world, my mind was quite at ease and I hoped that by that time, if I were not in the position to pay the sum myself, I should be able to borrow it. Well, Herr

von Tranner now informs me that the person in question absolutely refuses to wait and that if I do not pay the sum before tomorrow, he will 'bring an action against me'. Only think, your Ladyship, what an unpleasant business this would be for me! At the moment I cannot pay — not even half the sum!

As Wolfgang's artistic reputation grew, he felt the rivalry of other composers more and more. It was clear for example that Anton Salieri, first Kapellmeister at the Court Opera, feared his genius. Joseph Haydn, on the other hand, openly admired him and encouraged him all his life. The string quartet which Wolfgang finished in December 1782 was much influenced by Haydn's Russian string quartets. It was the first of six which he dedicated to the master in 1785 and on which he worked devotedly for a long time. No other manuscripts of his music show so many painstaking corrections.

I send my six sons to you, most celebrated and very dear friend. Please receive them kindly and be to them a father, guide and friend.

At the end of July 1783 Wolfgang and Constanze at last travelled to Salzburg to meet the family. They stayed till the autumn. On 26 October the Mass in C minor was performed for the first time at the Abbey of St. Peter. Constanze sang one of the soprano parts. This is how Wolfgang had vowed to celebrate his marriage and also his reunion with his father. Next morning he left with Constanze for Vienna by way of Linz.

The Burgtheater
on the Michaelerplatz,
Vienna, in Mozart's time

Neues Singspiel.

Die Kaiserl. Königl. National - Hof - Schauspieler
werden heute Dienstag den 16 July 1782 aufführen:

(Zum erstenmal)

Die Entführung aus dem Serail.

Ein Singspiel in drey Aufzügen,
nach Bretznern frey bearbeitet und für das k. k. Nationalhoftheater eingerichtet.

In Musik gesetzt vom Herrn Kapellmeister Mozart.

Die Bücher sind beym Logenmeister für 17. kr. zu haben.

Der Anfang ist um halb 7 Uhr.

Announcement of first performance of *The Abduction
from the Seraglio*

149

St. Stephans-Dom in Vienna where Wolfgang and Constanze were married

Constanze Mozart, *née* Weber. Oil painting by Hans Hansen, done in 1802, after Mozart's death

Joseph Haydn

Count
Esterházy

Title page of the six
string quartets
dedicated
to Joseph Haydn,
Vienna, 1785

SEI
QUARTETTI

PER DUE VIOLINI, VIOLA, E VIOLONCELLO.

Composti e Dedicati
al Signor

GIUSEPPE HAYDN

Maestro di Cappella di S. A.
il Principe d'Esterhazy &c. &c.
Dal Suo Amico

W. A. MOZART

Opera X.

Edmund Kozlowski

In Vienna presso Artaria Comp.
Mercanti ed Editori di Stampe Musica,
e Carte Geografiche.

Mozart's sons, Franz and Karl. Oil painting by Hans Hansen, c. 1798

'Zur Mehlgrube', Vienna, where Mozart often gave concerts

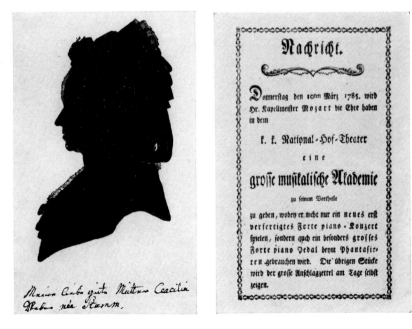

Cäcilia Weber, Mozart's mother-in-law   Announcement of a concert

Mozart's sister, Nannerl, after her marriage to Johann Baptist von Berchtold zu Sonnenburg.
Anonymous oil painting, c. 1785

During their nine years in Vienna, Wolfgang and Constanze moved house ten times, perhaps in search of lower rents, perhaps to escape creditors. First they moved to the Wipplingerstrasse, then into 'Haus Salzgries', on the Kohlmarkt, then to the Judenplatz, to the Trattnerhof, to a house in the Schulerstrasse — then the Landstrasse, into Tuchlauben, into the house 'Zum Auge Gottes', and again to the Judenplatz. Their last lodgings were in the Rauhensteingasse.

Wolfgang wrote less frequently to his father. He had no time. In the morning he gave lessons, in the evening he gave concerts. In the afternoons he composed. On 3 March 1784 he sent his father a list of his commitments:

March 4th, at Galitzin's — March 5th, at Esterházy's — March 8th, at Esterházy's — March 11th, at Galitzin's — March 12th, at Esterházy's — March 15th, at Esterházy's — March 17th, my first 'private' concert — March 18th, at Galitzin's — March 19th, at Esterházy's — March 20th, at Richter's — March 21st, my first concert 'in the theatre' . . .

Two weeks later he sent a list of the subscribers to his concerts. He put down 174 names and added: 'I alone have thirty more than Richter and Fischer together.'

By now Wolfgang had begun to note down the dates and titles of his compositions. He kept his 'Record of all my works' fairly accurately till the end of his life, and it is of course a valuable source of information about his later works. The titles of the compositions are followed by the opening bars. The first entries are:

1784 9th February a piano concerto. Accompaniment two violins, viola and bass. (two oboes, two horns ad libitum)

15th March a piano concerto. Accompaniment two violins, two violas, one flute, two oboes, two bassoons, two horns and bass.

22nd March a piano concerto. Accompaniment two violins, two violas, one flute, two oboes, two bassoons, two horns, two clarinets, timpani and bass.

30th March a piano quintet. Accompaniment one oboe, one clarinet, one horn and one bassoon.

In August of that year Nannerl married Johann Baptist von Berchtold zu Sonnenburg, a widower with five children, who was magistrate at St. Gilgen. Wolfgang sent his congratulations: 'And now I send you a thousand good wishes from Vienna to Salzburg, and hope particularly that you two will live together as harmoniously as — we two!'

To form an idea of what Wolfgang looked like at that time it is perhaps best to look at the portrait painted by his brother-in-law, Aloysia's husband, the actor Josef Lange. The picture, which was to have shown him at the piano, remained unfinished. Hieronymus Löschenkohl made a silhouette of his profile. Leonard Posch did a portrait in relief, Doris Stock a silverpoint drawing.

'He was small,' wrote Mozart's first biographer, Franz Xaver Niemetschek, 'and his countenance, excepting for the large fiery eyes, did not indicate the greatness of his genius.' According to his sister, he was 'small, thin, pale and quite devoid of all pretensions in his physiognomy and body'.

Leopold Mozart stayed with his son and daughter-in-law in Vienna from February till April 1785. He enjoyed Wolfgang's fame and wrote detailed letters about it to his daughter in St. Gilgen. He quoted Haydn, who had said to him:

> I tell you before God as an honest man, your son is the greatest composer whom I know personally or by repute; he has taste and what is more the most profound knowledge of composition.

Leopold went on to write about a concert:

> Your brother played a glorious concerto, and I had the great pleasure of hearing so clearly all the interplay of the instruments that for sheer delight tears came into my eyes. When your brother left the platform the Emperor waved his hat and called out 'Bravo, Mozart!'

He also kept an eye on his son's financial position:

> I believe, that if he has no debts to pay, my son could now put 2,000 florins into the bank. The money is certainly there — as regards food and drink the household is to the highest degree economical.

The 'Tonkünstler-Sozietät' did not accept Mozart as a member. The reason: He kept on forgetting to hand in his birth certificate. But the Freemasons admitted him to their ranks. The Lodge became for him the ideal of spiritual community and later he reached the degree of a master.

In a letter to the Privy Councillor Anton Klein in Mannheim he expressed his feelings about German opera:

> Were there but one good patriot in charge — things would take a different turn. But then, perhaps, the German national theatre which is sprouting so vigorously would actually begin to flower; and of course that would be an

everlasting blot on Germany, if we Germans were seriously to begin to think as Germans, to act as Germans, to speak German and, Heaven help us, to sing in German!!

Six months later Leopold remarked in a letter to Nannerl; that he had had no news from Wolfgang for six weeks but that there were rumours about a new opera. A little later he wrote: 'At last I have received a letter of twelve lines from your brother. He begs to be forgiven, as he is up to the eyes in work at his opera 'Le Nozze di Figaro'.

The libretto of *Le Nozze di Figaro* was based on a play by Beaumarchais which was at that time a sensational success. The play had opened in Paris in spite of strong opposition from the French king. By the time it reached the German stage it had been heavily censored, but the original text was available to those who could read French, and everybody talked about it. The Viennese talked about it too, although Joseph II would not permit its performance. It was only through the dexterity of Lorenzo da Ponte, Mozart's librettist, that the story was allowed to be put on as an opera. Instinctively, he knew how to make it acceptable. He wrote in his memoirs 'I have left out whole scenes, shortened others, trying always to omit anything that might offend propriety or good taste.'

Lorenzo da Ponte's own life was full with events that 'offended propriety'. He was born in the Venetian city of Ceneda in 1749, of Jewish parents, and was called Emanuele Conegliano until his fourteenth year when his father, a widower, wanting to marry a Christian girl, was received with his children into the Catholic Church. They were baptised by the Bishop of Ceneda, Lorenzo da Ponte, who gave his own name to the eldest boy. The new Lorenzo was persuaded to become a priest, but even after he was ordained he led a life of amorous adventure in Venice. Because of his radical views he was dismissed from the University of Treviso where he had become a teacher of rhetoric. Because of his libertine ways he was banished from the state of Venice altogether. That was why he went to Austria, where he was appointed poet to the Imperial Theatre in Vienna and where he worked with Mozart. But in 1790, when Joseph II died, he fell out of favour with the new Emperor Leopold II and after writing some scurrilous attacks on him he was banished from Vienna too. He lived for a time as a theatrical impresario and also a bookseller in London but owing to money difficulties had to flee to New York where he took up many trades including distilling and grocery. Eventually he became the first Professor of Italian at Columbia University and wrote his famous memoirs. He died in his ninetieth year in 1838.

On 11 February 1786 Mozart's singspiel in one act *Der Schauspieldirektor* was performed at the theatre next to the Kärntnertor. About ten weeks later on 1 May at the Burgtheater, the Viennese watched *Le Nozze di Figaro* for the first time. Some days later the *Wiener Realzeitung* gave it a long notice:

'What is not allowed to be said these days, is sung', one may say with Figaro. This piece, which was not allowed to be performed here as a comedy, we have at last had the felicity to see represented as an opera.

The public, however (and this often happens to the public) did not really know on the first day where it stood. It heard many a bravo from unbiased connoisseurs, but obstreperous louts in the uppermost storey exerted their hired lungs with all their might to deafen singers and audience alike with their St! and Pst!; and consequently opinions were divided at the end of the piece.

Apart from that, it is true that the first performance was none of the best, owing to the difficulty of the composition. But now, after several performances, one would be subscribing either to the cabal or to tastelessness if one were to maintain that Herr Mozart's music is anything but a masterpiece of art. It contains so many beauties, and such a wealth of ideas, as can be drawn only from the source of innate genius.

After nine performances *Le Nozze di Figaro*, despite its favourable reception by people qualified to judge it, was dropped. An intrigue of the cast? An intrigue of the courtiers? Certainly the social criticism contained in the work did not please the mighty.

Wolfgang wrote to his father:

If you are a rich ass, acquire land,

If you are an aristocratic but poor ass, do what you can for your bread.

If you are a rich aristocratic ass, become what you may, only not a man of intelligence, I beg you.

Silhouette
by
Hieronymus
Löschenkohl,
1785

Engraving, after the relief by Leonard Posch,
1789

Silverpoint drawing by Doris Stock,
1789

Mozart's 'Record of all my Works'

The first pages from the above

Mozart. Unfinished oil painting by Josef Lange, Mozart's brother-in-law, probably winter 1782—1783

The house in the Grosse Schulerstrasse where Mozart composed *The Marriage of Figaro*

(*Left*) Lorenzo da Ponte. (*Right*) The Overture, in Mozart's hand, with Andante crossed out

In Prague, on the other hand, *Le Nozze di Figaro* was a continuous success. The *Prager Oberpostamtszeitung* of 12 December 1786 confirmed this:

No piece (so everyone here asserts) has ever caused such a sensation as the Italian opera 'Le Nozze di Figaro', which has already been given several times here with unlimited applause by Bondini's resident company. The music is by our celebrated Herr Mozart. Connoisseurs who have seen this opera in Vienna are anxious to declare that it was done much better here. Our great Mozart must have heard about this himself, for there has been a rumour since that he will come here in person to see the piece.

Then an invitation reached Mozart from Prague 'where' it said, 'everyone longed to set eyes on the German Apollo.' The invitation assured him that he was awaited by 'an orchestra, and by a society of great connoisseurs and lovers of music.' On 11 January 1787 Wolfgang and Constanze arrived in Prague. They first put up at the Three Lions Inn, but the very next day moved to the palace of Count Thun. Four days after his arrival Wolfgang wrote to his friend Gottfried von Jacquin in Vienna:

At six o'clock I drove with Count Canal to the so-called Breitfeld ball, where the cream of the beauties of Prague is wont to gather. Why — you ought to have been there, my friend! I fancy I see you running, or rather, limping after all those pretty women, married and unmarried! I neither danced nor flirted with any of them, the former, because I was too tired, and the latter owing to my natural bashfulness. I looked on, however, with the greatest pleasure while all these people flew about in sheer delight to the music of my 'Figaro', arranged for quadrilles and waltzes. For here they talk about nothing but 'Figaro'. Nothing is played, sung or whistled but 'Figaro'. No opera is drawing like 'Figaro'. Nothing, nothing but 'Figaro'.

On 19 January he gave a concert at the Ständetheater. On the 22nd he conducted *Figaro* himself, and received tumultuous applause. When he left Prague he took with him a commission: the director of the theatre had asked him to write an opera for the following season.

Back in Vienna Mozart and Lorenzo da Ponte decided on *Don Giovanni*. Da Ponte is said to have told the Emperor: 'I shall write for Mozart, but will first read a few pages of Dante's *Inferno*, to find the right mood.'

While Wolfgang was composing *Don Giovanni* news arrived from Salzburg that his father was seriously ill. Leopold was sixty-seven years old. Wolfgang wrote to him on 4 April:

Now I hear that you are really ill. I need hardly tell you how greatly I am longing to receive some reassuring news from yourself. And I still expect it; although I have now made a habit of being prepared in all affairs of life for the worst. As death, when we come to consider it closely, is the true goal of our existence, I have formed during the last few years such close relations with this best and truest friend of mankind, that his image is not only no longer terrifying to me, but is indeed very soothing and consoling! And I thank my God for graciously granting me the opportunity (you know what I mean) of learning that death is the key which unlocks the door to our true happiness. I never lie down at night without reflecting that — young as I am — I may not live to see another day. Yet no one of all my acquaintances could say that in company I am morose or disgruntled. For this blessing I daily thank my Creator and wish with all my heart that each one of my fellow-creatures could enjoy it.

I hope and trust that while I am writing this, you are feeling better. But if, contrary to all expectation, you are not recovering, I implore you not to hide it from me, so that as quickly as is humanly possible I may come to your arms.

He did not see his father again. On 28 May 1787, early in the morning, Leopold Mozart died.

Pater Dominikus Hagenauer, Abbot of the Abbey of St. Peter in Salzburg and the son of his old friend from the Getreidegasse, wrote about Leopold in his diary:

He was a man of much wit and sagacity, who would have been capable of rendering good service to the State even apart from music. He was the most correct violinist of his time. He spent most of the days of his life in the service of the Court here, but had the misfortune of being always persecuted here and was not as much favoured by a long way as in other, larger places in Europe.

The contents of the Tanzmeisterhaus were auctioned. Wolfgang received 1,000 florins as his share of the proceeds.

In the autumn of 1787 Wolfgang and Constanze were again in Prague. The *Prager Oberpostamtszeitung* reported: 'Our celebrated Herr Mozart has again arrived in Prague, and the news has spread here since that the opera newly written by him, "Don Giovanni", will be given for the first time at the National Theatre'.

They lodged for a while at the Three Lions Inn and then went to stay with the famous singer Josepha Duschek and her husband, the pianist, at their

Villa Bertramka. Rehearsals began at which he and da Ponte were present, but there were many difficulties and the opening date kept on being postponed. Mozart told his friend Jacquin in a letter:

You probably think that my opera is over by now. If so, you are a little mistaken. In the first place, the stage personnel here are not as adept as those in Vienna, when it comes to mastering an opera of this kind in a very short time. Secondly, I found on my arrival that so few preparations and arrangements had been made that it would have been absolutely impossible to produce it on the 14th. *Don Giovanni* has now been fixed for the 24th.

Mozart did not send off the letter but added a few days later: 'It was fixed for the 24th, but a further postponement has been caused by the illness of one of the singers. My opera is to be performed for the first time on the 29th.'

Casanova came to watch the first performance. He was sixty-two then and lived a settled life near Prague as librarian to Count Waldstein. He had known da Ponte since his Venice days and there is evidence that he may have been consulted about the libretto. Two papers in his handwriting found after his death give a revised version of the situation after the sextet in the second act. His revision was not included in the opera.

The *Oberpostamtszeitung* reported on 3 November 1787:

On the 29th the Italian opera company gave the ardently awaited opera by Maestro Mozart, 'Don Giovanni, oder das steinerne Gastmahl'. Connoisseurs and musicians say that Prague had never yet heard the like. Herr Mozart conducted in person; when he entered the orchestra he was received with threefold cheers, which again happened when he left it. The opera is, moreover, extremely difficult to perform, and everyone admired the good performance given in spite of this after such a short period of study. Everybody, on the stage and in the orchestra, strained every nerve to thank Mozart by rewarding him with a good performance. There were also heavy additional costs, caused by several choruses and changes of scenery, all of which Herr Guardasoni had brilliantly attended to. The unusually large attendance testifies to a unanimous approbation.

To his friend Gottfried von Jacquin Mozart wrote: 'People here are doing their best to persuade me to remain on for a couple of months and write another opera. But I cannot accept this proposal, however flattering it may be.'

On 13 November he travelled back to Vienna with Constanze.

There on 15 November 1787 the Court composer Christoph Willibald von Gluck died. Mozart was appointed in his stead as Imperial Chamber Musician.

The Decree announcing his appointment is dated 1 December 1787:

From His Apostolic Majesty, Emperor of the Holy Roman Empire, King of Hungary and Bohemia, Archduke of Austria, &c. Our most gracious sovereign, concerning Wolfgang Mozart, graciously subjoins: that it has been H. I. & R. Apost. Maj.'s pleasure to do him the most signal honour of appointing him H. M. Kammermusikus, in view of his knowledge and capacity in music and the approbation he has earned thereby, and to condescend to command the I. & R. Treasury to assign him a salary of eight hundred florins per annum from 1 December of this year. In pursuance of which this Imperial resolution is herewith imparted to the said Wolfgang Mozart and the present decree of the High Chamberlain's Office drawn up at Imperial command as his guarantee.

As Court composer Gluck had received a yearly salary of 2,000 florins. Mozart was only paid 800, but then, unlike Gluck, he was not expected to compose symphonies and operas. He had only to write some dances each year for the masked balls of the Court. He wrote to his sister in St. Gilgen:

Of my writing *Don Giovanni* for Prague and of the opera's triumphant success you may have heard already, but that His Majesty the Emperor has now taken me into his service will probably be news to you. Write to me frequently. If I don't always answer promptly, put it down not to any negligence on my part, but simply to the many jobs which keep me busy.

His 'many jobs' took up much time but did not always bring in money. In his 'Record of all my works' the year 1788 starts off with an Allegro and Andante for piano solo, a country dance in D, 'Das Donnerwetter', a country dance in C, 'La bataille', and six German dances.

The Karlsbrücke in Prague

Thun Palace, Prague

The Ständetheater, Prague

Mozart's piano, built by Anton Walter in Vienna, c. 1780

Mozart's father. From the family portrait by della Croce

Leopold Mozart's gravestone in the churchyard of St. Sebastian, Salzburg

Prague with the Hradschin — the castle — in the background

Villa Bertramka, Prague

Don Giovanni. Canzonetta from the 2nd act, in Mozart's hand

174

After Mozart had for the time being turned down the offer to write a second opera for Prague, Franz Rott, one of the active patrons of music in Prague, approached Joseph Haydn. Haydn declined:

> I should be taking a great risk, since the great Mozart can scarcely have his equal. For if I were able to impress the soul of every music-lover with my own understanding of and feeling for Mozart's incomparable works, so profound and so full of musical intelligence, as my own sentiment dictates, then the nations would vie with each other to possess such a jewel within their encircling walls. Let Prague hold fast to the precious man — but also reward him.

Mozart's former successes in Vienna did not recur. People no longer waited eagerly for his next composition to appear. His new work was too difficult for amateurs to play, and at that time the piano sonata, the trio, the quartet and quintet were still mainly performed at home. The *Journal des Luxus und der Moden*, which was published in Weimar, appreciated this problem:

> Some time ago a quartet by him was engraved and published, which is very cunningly set and in performance needs the utmost precision in all the four parts, but even when well played, or so it seems, is able and intended to delight only connoisseurs of music in a musica di camera. This product of Mozart's can in truth hardly bear listening to when it falls into mediocre amateurish hands and is negligently played. Now this is what happened innumerable times last winter; at nearly every place my travels led me and where I was taken to a concert, some young lady or pretentious middle-class demoiselle, or some other pert dilettante in a noisy gathering, came up with this quartet and fancied that it would be enjoyed. But it could not please: everyone yawned with boredom. What a difference when this much-advertised work of art is performed with the highest degree of accuracy by four skilled musicians who have studied it carefully, in a quiet room where the suspension of every note cannot escape the listening ear.

On 7 May *Don Giovanni* had its first performance in Vienna. Mozart received two hundred and twenty-five florins. He had made some changes to please the Vienna public. Yet it was not a great success. The opera was performed fifteen times in 1788, then not again in his lifetime. The Emperor watched the last performance on 15 December. Da Ponte reported that he said: 'It is a divine work, even more beautiful than 'Figaro', but a hard nut for my Viennese!' Mozart is supposed to have added: 'Just give them time to chew.'

Mozart worked tirelessly, yet his situation grew worse. He could not manage on his salary as Imperial Chamber Musician. Constanze began to suffer from a foot complaint which made things more difficult because she needed expensive treatment. In June 1788 he wrote to the merchant Michael Puchberg, a freemason and brother at the same lodge: 'I still owe you eight ducats. Apart from the fact that at the moment I am not in a position to pay you back this sum, my confidence in you is so boundless that I dare to implore you to help me out with a hundred florins until next week.'

His friend made a note on the margin of the letter: 'Dispatched 100 florins'. A few days later Mozart wrote again to Puchberg:

The conviction that you are indeed my friend and that you know me to be a man of honour encourages me to open my heart to you completely and to make you the following request. If you have sufficient regard and friendship for me to assist me for a year or two one or two thousand florins, at a suitable rate of interest, you will help me enormously! If you will do me this kindness then, primo, as I shall have some money to go on with, I can meet necessary expenses whenever they occur, and therefore more easily, whereas now I have to postpone payments and then often at the most awkward time have to spend all I receive at one go; secondo, I can work with a mind more free from care and with a lighter heart, and thus earn more.

Puchberg noted on the letter: 'Sent 200 florins on 17th June.' Yet, in the same month, Mozart had to write a third letter:

My position is so serious that I am unavoidably obliged to raise money somehow. But, good God, in whom can I confide? In no one but you, my best friend! If you would only be so kind as to get the money for me through some other channel! I shall willingly pay the interest and whoever lends it to me will, I believe, have sufficient security in my character and my income.

Puchberg made no note on this one and at the beginning of July Mozart wrote again:

With great difficulty I have been able to manage my affairs so that all I need now is an advance on these two pawnbroker's tickets. In the name of our friendship I implore you to do me this favour; but you must do it immediately. Forgive my importunity, but you know my situation. Ah! If only you had done what I asked you! Do it even now — then everything will be as I desire. Ever your Mozart.

During those weeks — while he had to write such letters — he entered in the record of his works:

26th June	a symphony.	Two violins, one flute, two clarinets, two bassoons, two horns, two trumpets, timpani, violas and basses.
25th July	a symphony	Two violins, one flute, two oboes, two bassoons, two horns, violas and basses.
10th August	a symphony	Two violins, one flute, two oboes, two bassoons, two horns, two clarinets, **timpani**, violas and basses.

This group of his three last symphonies — in E flat major, G minor and C major — he composed in barely three months. At the same time he wrote also a trio for piano, violin and cello, a little march, a small piano sonata for beginners, a short Adagio ('for a fugue, which I wrote a long time ago for two pianos'), a small piano sonata for beginners with one violin, a trio for piano, violin and cello, a small canzonetta, a song ('Beim Auszug in das Feld').

In April he had advertised in the *Wiener Zeitung*: 'Three new Quintets which I offer by subscription, finely and correctly written.' Now in the summer he had to insert the announcement: 'As the number of subscribers is still very small, I find myself obliged to postpone the publication of my three Quintets until 1st January 1789.'

The three quintets (for two violins, two violas and cello) appeared separately after Mozart's death. After the summer of 1788 he did not write any more symphonies, only one piano concerto. Also, he held no more public concerts.

In the diary of a Danish actor, Joachim Daniel Preisler, who had been sent to study the theatre in Vienna, there is a description of a visit to the Mozart household in August 1788:

There I had the happiest hour of music that has ever fallen to my lot. This small man and great master twice extemporized on a pedal pianoforte, so wonderfully that I quite lost myself. He intertwined the most difficult passages with the most lovely themes. — His wife cut quill-pens for the copyist, a pupil composed, a little boy aged four walked about in the garden and sang recitatives — in short, everything that surrounded this splendid man was musical!

In March, 1789, Mozart wrote to his friend Franz Hofdemel, Clerk of the Supreme Judiciary in Vienna:

Dearest friend, I am taking the liberty of asking you without any hesitation for a favour. I should be very much obliged to you it you could and would lend me a hundred florins until the 20th of next month. On that day I receive the quarterly instalment of my salary and shall then repay the loan with thanks.

Hofdemel lent him the hundred florins — for four months against a bill of exchange which Mozart agreed to 'duly pay on expiration and submit myself to the Imperial Mercantile and Exchange Court.'

Prince Karl Lichnowsky, who was about to make a journey to Berlin, had invited Mozart to accompany him and with this borrowed money he accepted the offer, hoping to find a better position there and solve his difficulties. On 8 April they left Vienna together. In Budwitz, where they spent the first night of their long journey, Wolfgang wrote his first letter to Constanze:

Dearest little wife! While the Prince is busy bargaining about horses, I am delighted to seize this opportunity to write a few lines to you, dearest little wife of my heart. How are you? I wonder whether you think of me as often as I think of you? Every moment I look at your portrait — and weep partly for you, partly for sorrow. Look after your health which is so precious to me and fare well, my darling! Do not worry about me, for I am not suffering any discomforts or annoyance on this journey — apart from your absence — which, as it can't be helped, can't be remedied. I write this note with eyes full of tears. Adieu. I shall write a longer and more legible letter to you from Prague, for then I shan't have to hurry so much. Adieu. I kiss you millions of times most tenderly and am ever yours, true till death,

Mozart.

Masked ball in the Redoutensaal, the Assembly room, of the palace in Vienna

Title-page of the Masonic Cantata 'Die Maurerfreude'

Mozart's announcement in the *Wiener Zeitung*. His quintets cannot be published for lack of subscribers

One of Mozart's appeals to Michael Puchberg. Underneath it on the left, Puchberg's note of the sum he sent him

The first page of the Rondo in A minor

They travelled via Prague to Dresden. Here Mozart gave a private concert and played at the Elector's court — for which, as in his early days, he received a snuff-box. He also engaged in a trial of skill with the famous organist Hässler in the court church.

In Leipzig he played on the orgen of St. Thomas's Church where Johann Sebastian Bach had been organist and choirmaster for nearly thirty years. There he discovered the manuscript of Bach's cantata 'Sing to the Lord a new song'. He studied it closely, realising how much he could learn from Bach.

On 25 April Mozart and Lichnowsky arrived in Potsdam. Mozart wanted 'to lay his talents at his Sovereign Majesty's feet'. His Sovereign Majesty the King of Prussia, Friedrich Wilhelm II, would not receive him, but sent a message telling him to get in touch with Duport, the Director of Chamber Music. Mozart then wrote some piano variations on a minuet by Duport, but nothing more happened.

Prince Lichnowsky now wanted to return to Leipzig. Mozart went with him and gave a concert 'for his own benefit' but the profits were meagre.

His last hope was that King Friedrich Wilhelm would receive him in Berlin. There Mozart watched a performance of his *Seraglio* and then, finally, on 26 May he did play at the palace. He was asked to write six piano sonatas and six string quartets but was not offered a post.

Two days later he set off on his return journey to Vienna and on 4 June he was back at home. He had written twelve letters to Constanze.

From Dresden, at half past eleven at night:

Then came the happiest of all moments for me. I found a letter from you, that letter which I had longed for so ardently, my darling, my beloved! I immediately went off in triumph to my room, kissed the letter countless times before breaking the seal, and then devoured it rather than read it.

Dear little wife, I have a number of requests to make. I beg you 1. not to be melancholy,

2. to take care of your health and to beware of the spring breezes.

3. not to go out walking alone — and preferably not to go out walking at all,

4. to feel absolutely assured of my love. Up to the present I have not written a single letter to you without placing your dear portrait before me.

5. I beg you in your conduct not only to be careful of your honour and mine, but also to consider appearances. Do not be angry with me for asking this. You ought to love me even more for thus valuing our honour.

6. and lastly I beg you to send me more details in your letters.

From Leipzig:

I wanted to get away yesterday, but could find no horses. I am having the same difficulty today. For at the present moment everyone is trying to get off, and the number of travellers is simply enormous. But we shall be on the road tomorrow at five o'clock. I received in Leipzig on April 21st your letter of April 13th. Then I spent seventeen days in Potsdam without any letters.

From Berlin:

This time I can't write very much to you, as I have to pay some calls and I am only sending you this to announce my arrival. Oh, how glad I shall be to be with you again, my darling. But the first thing I shall do is to take you by your front curls; for how on earth could you think, or even imagine, that I had forgotten you? How could I possibly do so?

Four days later, again from Berlin:

My darling little wife, when I return you must be more delighted with having me back than with the money I shall bring. A hundred friedrichs d'or are not nine hundred florins but seven hundred — at least that is what they told me here. Secondly, Lichnowsky (as he was in a hurry) left me here and so I have had to pay for my keep in this expensive place. Thirdly, I had to lend him a hundred florins, as his purse was getting empty, I could not well refuse him. Fourthly, my concert at Leipzig was a failure, as I always said it would be.

From Prague: 'God, I am so happy to be seeing you again!'
All his travel and exertion had hardly brought in anything. Again and again he had to turn to his friend Puchberg:

Great God! I would not wish my worst enemy to be in my present position. And if you, most beloved friend and brother, forsake me, we are altogether lost, both my unfortunate and blameless self and my poor sick wife and child. Only the other day when I was with you I was longing to open my heart to you. Good God! I am coming to you not with thanks but with fresh entreaties!

During the eight years that Mozart had now spent in Vienna, he had written over two hundred works. But in the summer of 1789 a correspondent from Copenhagen reported that in Vienna: 'Mozart's works do not in general please quite so much. He has a decided leaning towards the difficult and the unusual.' Yet, everywhere else his music was in demand.

In the year 1789 'a music-loving public' — as it said in the announcements of the time — heard:

in Dresden	A suite for wind from *Don Giovanni*
in Mainz	*La finta giardiniera*
	Don Giovanni
in Bamberg	*Die Entführung aus dem Serail*
in Frankfurt	*La finta giardiniera*
	Don Giovanni
in Hannover	*Le Nozze di Figaro*
in Dresden	the piano concerto in C major
in Ofen	*Die Entführung aus dem Serail*
in Hamburg	*Die Entführung aus dem Serail*
in Braunschweig	*Le Nozze di Figaro*
in Berlin	*Die Entführung aus dem Serail*
in Bonn	*Don Giovanni*
in Warsaw	*Don Giovanni*
in Frankfurt	*Le Nozze di Figaro*
in Hamburg	*Don Giovanni*
in Kassel	Symphonies
in Mainz	*Le Nozze di Figaro*
in Graz	*Don Giovanni*
in Brünn	*Don Giovanni*

For all those performances Mozart received not a penny. It was in the days before copyright.

He wrote to his friend Puchberg:

I fear you are angry with me, for you are not sending me a reply! When I compare the proofs of your friendship with my present demands upon it, I cannot but admit that you are perfectly right. But when I compare my misfortunes (for which I am not to blame) with your kindly disposition towards me, then I do find that there is some excuse for me. As in my last letter to you, my dear friend, I told you quite frankly everything that was burdening my heart, I can only repeat today what I said then. But I must still add that (1) I should not require such a considerable sum if I did not anticipate very heavy expenses in connection with the cure my wife may have to take, particularly if she has to go to Baden. (2) As I am positive that in a short time I shall be in better circumstances, the amount of the sum I shall have to repay is a matter of indifference to me. Nevertheless at the present moment I should prefer it to be a large sum.

Puchberg noted on the letter: 'answered the same day, 17 July 1789, and sent 150 florins.'

In his own words, Mozart lived 'between fear and hope'. Constanze's foot had not got better, and the doctor recommended a cure at the sulphur springs in Baden. Wolfgang wrote to her there. Judging by his letter she seemed to have enjoyed her stay:

> I want to talk to you quite frankly. You have no reason whatever to be unhappy. You have a husband who loves you and does all he possibly can for you. As for your foot, you must be patient and it will surely get well again. I am glad indeed when you have some fun — of course I am — but I do wish that you would not sometimes make yourself so cheap. In my opinion you are too free and easy with N. N. Now please remember that N. N. are not half so familiar with other women, whom they perhaps know more intimately, as they are with you. Why, N. N. who is usually a well-conducted fellow and particularly respectful to women, must have been misled by your behaviour into writing the most disgusting and most impertinent sottises in his letter. A woman must always make herself respected. Remember that you yourself once admitted to me that you were inclined to comply too easily.

In the middle of August Mozart joined Constanze for two days in Baden to talk it over with her. He was in a hurry to return to Vienna because *Le Nozze di Figaro* was to be revived at the Burgtheater. He had written two new arias for it and attended the rehearsals.

In the year 1789 he only entered sixteen works in his records, including the clarinet quintet which he had written for his friend Anton Stadler. His last letter that year was again directed to Michael Puchberg:

> Do not be alarmed at the contents of this letter. Only to you, most beloved friend, who know everything about me and my circumstances, have I the courage to open my heart completely. According to the present arrangement I am to receive from the management next month two hundred ducats for my opera. If you can lend me four hundred florins until then, you will be rescuing your friend from the greatest embarrassment.

The Hofkirche,
Dresden

S. Thomas Kirche.

The Church
of St. Thomas,
Leipzig

The old market, Potsdam

Friedrich Wilhelm II,
King of Prussia

188

The Schlossplatz, Berlin

Mozart's signature

On 26 January 1890, *Così fan tutte* had its first performance at the Burg-theater. Some say that the Emperor, who had commissioned it, had himself suggested the plot and that it was based on incidents which had actually taken place in Viennese court circles. The libretto was by Lorenzo da Ponte. Its success was moderate. The *Wiener Zeitung* merely announced without comment that it had taken place. The Weimar paper *Journal des Luxus und der Moden* confined itself to the statement 'That the music is by Mozart says, I believe, everything.' *Così fan tutte* was performed ten times.

The Emperor Joseph II died on 20 February. When his brother Leopold succeeded him Lorenzo da Ponte had to go. He had not only been Mozart's librettist and friend, but also an intermediary between him and the Imperial Theatre. It was a hard blow when he had to leave Vienna.

Up to August Mozart had to ask his friend Puchberg nine times for money. Not once was he refused, as the notes on the margins of the letters show.

20 January	sent a hundred florins
20 February	sent twenty-five florins
End of March	sent one hundred and fifty florins
8 April	sent twenty-five florins
23 April	sent twenty-five florins
Beginning of May	sent a hundred florins
17 May	sent one hundred and fifty florins
12 June	sent twenty-five florins
14 August	sent ten florins

Mozart also asked him to help in other ways: 'I have two pupils and should very much like to raise the number to eight. Do your best to spread the news that I am willing to give lessons'. Often he felt almost at the end of his strength:

Whereas I felt tolerably well yesterday, I am absolutely wretched today. I could not sleep all night for pain. I must have got overheated yesterday from walking so much and then without knowing it have caught a chill. Picture yourself my conditions — ill and consumed by worries and anxieties. Such a state quite definitely prevents me from recovering. In a week or a fortnight I shall be better off certainly, but at present I am in want! Can you not help me out with a trifle? The smallest sum would be very welcome just now. You would, for the moment at least, bring peace of mind to your true friend, servant and brother   W. A. Mozart.

Puchberg noted down: 'sent, on 14 August 1790, ten florins'.

There were only two new entries in the record of his work during the first six months of the year — two string quartets, one in May, one in June. They were intended for the King of Prussia.

In search for a more remunerative post he petitioned the Archduke Franz:

I make so bold as to beg your Royal Highness very respectfully to use your most gracious influence with His Majesty the King with regard to my most humble petition to His Majesty. Prompted by a desire for fame, by a love of work and by a conviction of my wide knowledge, I venture to apply for the post of second Kapellmeister, particularly as Salieri, that very gifted Kapellmeister, has never devoted himself to church music, whereas from my youth up I have made myself completely familiar with this style. The slight reputation I have acquired in the world by my pianoforte playing, has encouraged me to ask His Majesty for the favour of being entrusted with the musical education of the Royal Family.

Whether the petition was ever sent is uncertain but in any case nothing came of it.

In the summer Constanze went again to Baden.

Dearest little wife, I trust that you have received my letter. Well, I must scold you a little, my love! Even if it is not possible for you to get a letter from me, you could write all the same; for must all your letters be replies to mine? I was most certainly expecting a letter from my dear little wife — but unfortunately I was mistaken.

In October Leopold II was to be crowned in Frankfurt. Mozart had hoped to be one of his official retinue but found himself excluded and had to make the journey at his own expense. The Emperor was attended by Salieri — Mozart was merely an onlooker at the Coronation. *Don Giovanni*, which was to have been performed, was cancelled and Dittersdorf's *Die Liebe im Narrenhaus* done instead. A concert he gave was disappointing. It brought in little money. Also it was too long and the audience left before the end. Mozart's final symphony had to be dropped from the programme. A second concert which he had planned did not take place.

He made his way back to Vienna via Mainz, Mannheim, Schwetzingen, Augsburg and Munich. While the *Historisch-Biographische Lexikon der Tonkünstler* for the year 1790, a kind of *Who's Who* in music, printed the fiction that he was drawing a yearly salary of 6,000 florins, Mozart, on 1 October, signed the following promissory note:

I, the undersigned, Wolfgang A. Mozart, Court Composer of this place, herewith declare and acknowledge for myself and for my heirs and assigns officially and in due legal form, that Herr Heinrich Lackenbacher, licensed merchant of this place, has lent me at my request and my then need, and paid me in cash without any deduction whatever, a capital of 1,000 florins. I therefore not only acknowledge herewith due receipt of this loan, but also bind myself and my heirs and assigns to repay this capital to the above-named lender or his heirs and assigns at the end of two years a dato, without preliminary notice and in the same coinage described above, without exception of any kind, and in the meantime to pay interest at five per cent in the same currency, which interest to be punctually paid here in Vienna in half-yearly instalments, failing which I am to forfeit the term of repayment of the capital and the lender may at once redemand the same with full interest and costs.

As security for both the capital and the interest I pledge the lender all my goods and chattels.

In witness whereof my and the invited witnesses' own hands. Enacted in Vienna on 1st October 1790.

Mathias Brünner	Anton Heindl	W. A. Mozart
witness	witness	

That same month an invitation reached him from London: to come for six months and write two operas — for which Robert May O'Reilly, the manager of an Italian company, offered him three hundred pounds. We do not know whether Mozart even answered the invitation.

In his 'Record of all my works' he made only two further entries that year: a quintet, and a piece for a musical-clock. In January 1791 he had again to write music for the Court balls: minuets, German dances, country dances etc.

To escape from his desperate condition he applied to the city of Vienna:

Most Honourable and most Learned Municipal Councillors of Vienna! Most Worthy Gentlemen! When Kapellmeister Hofmann was ill, I thought of venturing to apply for his post, seeing that my musical talents, my works and my skill in composition are well known in foreign countries, my name is treated everywhere with some respect, and I myself was appointed several years ago composer to the distinguished Court of Vienna. I trusted therefore that I was not unworthy of this post and that I deserved the favourable consideration of our enlightened municipal council.

Kapellmeister Hofmann, however, has recovered his health and in the circumstances — for I wish him from my heart a long life — it has occurred to me that it might perhaps be of service to the Cathedral and, most worthy gentlemen, to your advantage, if I were to be attached for the time being as unpaid assistant to this ageing Kapellmeister and were to have the opportunity of helping this worthy man in his office, thus gaining the approbation of our municipal council by the actual performance of services which I may justly consider myself peculiarly fitted to render on account of my thorough knowledge of both the secular and ecclesiastical styles of music.

Your most humble servant

Wolfgang Amadé Mozart
Royal and Imperial Court Composer.

The application was granted — but Hofmann continued in good health.

In June Constanze again went to Baden for a cure. Wolfgang visited her — but could not stay: he was working on an opera. On his return to Vienna, he sent her a touching testimony of his love:

When I think how merry we were together at Baden — like children — and what sad, weary hours I am spending here! Even my work gives me no pleasure, because I am accustomed to stop working now and then and exchange a few words with you. Alas! this pleasure is no longer possible.

He entered into his 'Record', *Die Zauberflöte* and — he had only begun the work in August — *La Clemenza di Tito*. In September he wrote to an unknown correspondent, probably Lorenzo da Ponte:

I feel it, and my condition tells me: The hour has struck! I must die. I am at an end now, before I could enjoy my talent. Life was so beautiful. It began so auspiciously! But one cannot alter one's destined fate. No one can safeguard his days. We have to submit to the will of providence.

Mozart travelled to Prague to conduct *La Clemenza di Tito*, commissioned for the Coronation of Leopold as King of Bohemia. It was not a success. But *Die Zauberflöte* was.

Emanuel Schikaneder, the director of the 'Theatre on the Wieden' who was a freemason like Mozart, wrote the libretto. Mozart assisted him. Schikander knew what the public on the outskirts of Vienna wished to see: a mixture of myth and fairytale, sublime and gay. Beauty, greatness, divine innocence, — a representation of masonic thought. Mozart expressed it in his music, great parts of which he wrote in the Summerhouse of the Starhemberg family.

The opera opened on 30 September, 1791, at the Theatre on the Wieden, Mozart conducted from the pianoforte and three brother masons sang the main parts: Schack sang Tamino, Gerl Sarastro, Schikaneder Papageno. It was slow to catch on but gradually became the most popular opera in Vienna. It was the greatest triumph in Mozart's life. In October alone it was performed twenty-four times. By November 1792 it had had a hundred performances, three years later two hundred.

In October Constanze returned to Baden. Mozart wrote to her:

> I have this moment returned from the opera, which was as full as ever. As usual the duet 'Mann und Weib' and Papageno's glockenspiel in Act I had to be repeated and also the trio of the boys in Act II. But what always gives me most pleasure is the silent approval. You can see how this opera is becoming more and more esteemed.

The following night he told her about the next performance:

> During Papageno's aria with the glockenspiel I went behind the scenes, as I felt a sort of impulse today to play it myself. Well, just for fun, at the point where Schikaneder has a pause, I played an arpeggio. He was startled, looked behind the wings and saw me. When he had his next pause, I played no arpeggio. This time he stopped and refused to go on. I guessed what he was thinking and again played a chord. He then struck the glockenspiel and said 'Shut up'. Whereupon everyone laughed. I am inclined to think that this joke taught many of the audience for the first time that Papageno does not play the instrument himself.

On 13 October Mozart invited the Court Kapellmeister Salieri and the singer Caterina Cavalieri to the performance. 'You can hardly imagine how charming they were', he wrote to Constanze, 'and how much they liked not only my music, but the libretto and everything. They both said that it was an "Operone", worthy to be performed for the grandest festival and before the greatest monarch . . . '

While *The Magic Flute* was being performed almost daily at the Theatre on the Wieden, Mozart was working on the Requiem. In the summer Count Walsegg-Stuppach's bailiff had called on him anonymously and commissioned a requiem, which the Count wished to have performed in memory of his late wife. It was to be announced as the Count's own composition. Mozart had accepted the commission on these terms. He never finished the work. While he was employed on it he also composed a 'Little Masonic Cantata' and on 18 November conducted its performance. Two days later he was so ill that he had to take to his bed. But he did not stop composing. He told his friends who came to visit him that it was his own Requiem he was writing.

194

Many years later Sophie Haibel, Constanze's youngest sister, recalled the last days of her brother-in-law:

Well, Mozart became fonder and fonder of our dear departed mother and she of him. Indeed he often came running along in great haste to the Wieden (where she and I were lodging at the Golden Plow), carrying under his arm a little bag containing coffee and sugar, which he would hand to our good mother, saying: 'Here, mother dear, now you can have a nice cup of coffee.' She used to be as delighted as a child. He did this very often. In short, Mozart never came to see us without bringing something.

Now when Mozart fell ill we both made him a night jacket which he could put on frontways, since on account of his swollen condition he was unable to turn in bed. Then, as we didn't know how seriously ill he was, we also made him a quilted dressing-gown, so that when he got up he should have everything he needed. We often visited him.

Once on a Sunday: I said to our good mother: 'Dear Mamma, I'm not going to see Mozart today. He was so well yesterday.' . . . She said: 'Go into town and bring me back news of him at once. But be sure not to delay.' I hurried along as fast as I could. Alas, how frightened I was when my sister came out to me almost in despair and said: 'Thank God that you have come, dear Sophie. Last night he was so ill that I thought he would not be alive this morning.' I tried to control myself and went to his bedside. He immediately called me to him and said: 'Ah, dear Sophie, how glad I am that you have come. You must stay here tonight and see me die.' I tried hard to be brave and to persuade him to the contrary. But to all my attempts he only replied: 'Why, I have already the taste of death on my tongue . . .'

I ran off to my mother who was anxiously awaiting me. Poor soul, how shocked she was! I persuaded her to go and spend the night with her eldest daughter. I then ran back as fast as I could to my distracted sister. Süssmayr was at Mozart's bedside. The well-known Requiem lay on the quilt and Mozart was explaining to him how, in his opinion, he ought to finish it when he was gone.

On Monday, 5 December 1791, at five minutes to one in the morning, Mozart died. The medical diagnosis at the time was 'heated miliary fever'. Of the many theories since advanced perhaps the most convincing is uraemia, but no one has ever ascertained the real cause of death.

On 6 December at three o'clock in the afternoon the body was blessed at the Stephansdom and taken to the St. Marx cemetery. There it was buried with others in a common grave as was usual for the poor in those days. His widow was not present. Mozart's grave is unknown.

Così fan tutte. The beginning of the second act, in Mozart's hand

La Clemenza di Tito, in Mozart's hand

The Magic Flute. Tamino's aria in the first act, in Mozart's hand

The summerhouse in the Starhembergs' garden

Emanuel Schikaneder

The last bars Mozart wrote — the Lacrimosa from the 'Requiem'

ACKNOWLEDGEMENTS

The authors wish to express their indebtedness to the new edition of the complete works of Mozart, published for the International Mozarteum Foundation, Salzburg, by Bärenreiter Verlag: also to the four-volume *Letters and Documents*, edited by Wilhelm A. Bauer and Otto Erich Deutsch, *Mozart and His Time, in Contemporary Pictures* and '*Mozart — A Documentary Biography*' both by Otto Erich Deutsch, and to the translators, Eric Blom, Peter Branscombe and Jeremy Noble, and the publisher, A & C Black, for permission to quote from the English edition of the last mentioned work.

The authors are also indebted to the estate of the late Emily Anderson and to Macmillan and Company Ltd. and St Martin's Press, Inc. for permission to quote from *The Letters of Mozart and His Family* translated and edited by Emily Anderson.

In addition to these works a vast number of other sources have been consulted, a list of which the authors feel would be too extensive for a volume intended for the the general reader. The illustrations are based on the film THE LIFE OF MOZART, for which new photographs were taken even of the most familiar and frequently reproduced portraits, documents and places. Here again it would be impracticable to give a complete list of the sources. We would, however, like to extend our special thanks to

Die Bayerische Staatsbibliothek, Munich
Die Bayerische Verwaltung der Staatlichen Schlösser, Gärten und Seen
La Bibliothèque Nationale, Paris
The British Museum, London
Die Deutsche Mozartgesellschaft
Die Graphische Sammlung Albertina, Vienna
The International Mozarteum Foundation, Salzburg
Das Kunsthistorische Museum, Vienna
Die Mozart-Gedenkstätten Salzburg und Augsburg
Die Österreichische Nationalbibliothek, Vienna
Die Residenz Salzburg
Das Salzburger Landesarchiv
Das Salzburger Museum Carolino Augusteum
Die Staatliche Graphische Sammlung, Munich
Das Städtische Reiss-Museum, Mannheim
Das Stadtarchiv, Augsburg
Das Stadtmuseum, Munich
Die Universitätsbibliothek, Tübingen

In addition to our own material, we have reproduced from the film photographs by Josef Dapra, and Manfred Mayr.